APEX maths

3

Extension *for all* through problem solving

Teacher's Handbook

Year 3 / Primary 4

Ann Montague-Smith

Paul Harrison

CAMBRIDGE
UNIVERSITY PRESS

PUBLISHED BY THE PRESS SYNDICATE OF THE UNIVERSITY OF CAMBRIDGE
The Pitt Building, Trumpington Street, Cambridge, United Kingdom

CAMBRIDGE UNIVERSITY PRESS
The Edinburgh Building, Cambridge CB2 2RU, UK
40 West 20th Street, New York, NY 10011–4211, USA
477 Williamstown Road, Port Melbourne, VIC 3207, Australia
Ruiz de Alarcón 13, 28014 Madrid, Spain
Dock House, The Waterfront, Cape Town 8001, South Africa

http://www.cambridge.org

First published 2003

Printed in Dubai by Oriental Press

Typefaces Frutiger, Swift   *System* QuarkXPress® 4.03

A catalogue record for this book is available from the British Library

ISBN 0 521 75491 7 paperback

Authors Ann Montague-Smith, Paul Harrison

ACKNOWLEDGEMENTS
Content editing by Beverley Uttley
Cover design by Karen Thomas
Text illustration by Beccy Blake
Project management by Cambridge Publishing Management Limited
The authors and publishers would like to thank the schools and individuals who trialled lessons.

Contents

Introduction

Lesson plans

Introduction

About Apex Maths

Apex Maths uses problem solving to address the needs of the more able and also provides extension and enrichment opportunities for children of all abilities. This allows Apex Maths to be used within the context of the whole-class daily mathematics lesson, reflecting the philosophy of the National Numeracy Strategy *Framework for teaching mathematics*.

Thirty detailed lesson plans are presented in the Teacher's Handbook. Each focuses on a core problem or investigation that is differentiated in various ways so that children of all abilities can work at their level on the same basic problem.

The lessons address all the problem solving objectives in the *Framework* and span all *Framework* strands.

The problems are richer and deeper than the relatively straightforward word problems suggested by the *Framework* examples, thereby helping children to develop thinking skills. They provide contexts in which children can apply and extend their mathematical skills and understanding, and consolidate their problem solving skills.

The teaching approach adopted throughout allows children to use enquiry, creative thinking and reasoning skills to solve a problem, with input from the teacher in the form of probing questions and occasional suggestions and hints. A carefully designed plenary encourages children to discuss their reasoning and evaluate the strategies used.

Teacher's materials

The Teacher's Handbook includes:

Scope and sequence chart
This lists all the problems together with the problem solving objectives addressed (from the *Framework for teaching mathematics*), the likely outcome levels for each ability group for Attainment Target 1 (Using and applying mathematics) in the *National Curriculum for England: mathematics* and the *Framework* topics addressed by each problem.

Scotland 5–14 Guidelines
A chart linking each lesson to related strands in *Curriculum and Assessment in Scotland, National Guidelines: Mathematics 5–14*.

Northern Ireland Lines of Development
A table linking each lesson to related *Northern Ireland Lines of Development* (levels 2 and 3).

Oral and mental problem solving starters
A bank of oral and mental starters with a problem solving slant, which can be used at the start of any lesson.

Lesson plans
These are presented in double-page spreads. A blueprint on pages 8–9 explains the features of the plans.

The lesson plans feature different types of problems, including:

- investigations requiring the identification of patterns and the making of generalisations;
- number puzzles and investigations that require reasoning about numbers;
- 'real-life' multi-stage problems involving a range of mathematical techniques;
- word problems where combinations of known values are used to find unknown values.

Useful mathematical information
This is a bank of additional mathematical information. It might explain a particular concept or look at a particular problem in greater depth.

Pupils' materials

Problems are presented for children in the Pupil's Textbook and/or using Photocopy Masters (PCMs) from the Teacher's Handbook.

Where parts of the page are numbered in the Textbook, this generally indicates a progression in the complexity of the problem. The **Differentiation** section in the Lesson plan indicates which parts of the pupil material are intended for which ability group.

Sometimes differentiation of a problem involves giving clues or additional direction to the Average or Less able groups.

Within the Textbook a blue tinted box indicates text which all children should read.

Equipment needed by children is shown in red text.

The Textbook also contains a glossary of mathematical and problem solving terms used in the problems.

Approaches to problem solving

When working at solving problems, children benefit from discussing what they have to do and how they might go about this. This can be as part of a whole-class discussion, or in pairs or small groups. On occasions, the discussion may not appear to be contributing to the resolution of the problem, but it can be allowed to continue for a short while so that children gain confidence in putting forward their ideas and using mathematical vocabulary appropriately.

Problem solving offers excellent opportunities to develop thinking and reasoning skills. This should be encouraged so that children become confident in using these skills not just when involved in problem solving, but in all their mathematical work and in other curriculum areas. Children should be encouraged to:

- choose the appropriate mathematics for the problem, and explain why they made their choice;
- be confident to try different strategies, evaluate their effectiveness and recognise when their chosen strategy is not effective;
- draw a picture or diagram or use equipment to aid understanding;
- try a simpler case in order to understand how the problem could be solved;

- work in a systematic way, recording work in a logical order, so that it is clear to others what has been tried;
- look for a pattern;
- form hypotheses, asking and answering questions such as 'What if ...?';
- consider if there are other, and better, solutions;
- try extensions to the problem, asking and answering 'What could I try next?';
- report what they have done in order to solve the problem, speaking clearly, and using appropriate mathematical vocabulary.

Because children approach problems from different perspectives, including different experiences of mathematics and varying degrees of understanding, it is important to accept a range of strategies for solving a problem and a variety of solutions. By making a comfortable atmosphere where it is safe to put forward a view, idea, or solution, children's confidence in their problem solving abilities will increase. It is also important to follow a problem through to a satisfactory solution so that children can learn from others, and improve their understanding of what is expected from them and ways of going about finding solutions. Expect your successes to improve as children's experience and confidence increases.

Sometimes when you ask a question, children will not respond immediately. Make use of silence; give children time to think through what has been asked so that they can formulate a response.

Lesson timing

The problem solving lessons in Apex Maths are designed to last for the length of a normal daily maths lesson. However, children's response to a given problem may determine whether the lesson could be extended for some minutes or returned to in another maths lesson.

Features of the lesson plans

Resources

Any Textbook pages, PCMs, and equipment needed by the teacher, plus resources that children might choose to use, depending upon the problem solving approach they decide to take.

Key vocabulary

The main problem solving and mathematical terms associated with the problem.

What's the problem?

A brief description of the problem and the mathematics that might be encountered, bearing in mind that children may use different areas of mathematics to solve the problem in their own way.

Problem solving objectives

The key problem solving objectives for the lesson.

Differentiation

Suggested activities for different ability groups. Children should not feel restricted to one activity and should, where appropriate, be allowed to move on to a more demanding activity.

Introducing the problem

Ideas for introducing the problem to children before they consider their strategy and begin the investigation.

Minimum prior experience

The minimum mathematical experience required for children to participate in the lesson. This will help you to decide when in the year to use each lesson.

---

20 Money box

Minimum prior experience

simple fractions; finding totals of coins

Resources

Textbook page 30, a selection of coins for each pair of children, to match the type of coins in their problem

Key vocabulary

part, equal parts, fraction, one whole, half, quarter, third, pound, penny, value, worth

---

What's the problem?

Children use their knowledge and understanding of fractions to calculate the total value of some given coins. They calculate $\frac{1}{2}$, $\frac{1}{4}$ or $\frac{1}{3}$ of numbers, depending on their ability (see **Differentiation**).

Problem solving objectives

- Choose and use appropriate number operations and appropriate ways of calculating to solve word problems.
- Explain methods and reasoning orally and, where appropriate, in writing.
- Solve mathematical problems or puzzles, recognise simple patterns and relationships, generalise and predict. Suggest extensions by asking 'What if . . .?'

Differentiation

The problem is differentiated by the fractions of questions calculated:

More able: Problem 3: thirds (of 24)

Average: Problem 2: quarters (of 12)

Less able: Problem 1: halves (of 10)

Introducing the problem

Ask children to look at their textbook page. *You are told some information about which coins are in a money box. Now you have to work out how much money there is in total.* Remind children that they will be using their knowledge and understanding of fractions.

60

Check that each ability group reads their specific problem on the page.

Explain that you are interested in how children work out their answer, and in how they record their work. Ask children to decide with a partner how they will begin, then start the problem.

Teacher focus for activity

All children: Check that children remember how many of the fractional parts given make one whole. Check that children understand that one whole refers to the total number of coins in the money box, and not the value of the coins.
As children work ask questions such as:

- *What is one half . . . quarter . . . third . . . of . . .?*
- *How did you work that out?*
- *How many coins are left? How do you know that?*

More able: Ask children to calculate $\frac{1}{3}$ of 24. Agree that this is how many £1 and how many 50p coins there are.

Average: Ask children to calculate $\frac{1}{4}$ of 12. Agree that this is how many 10p and how many 50p coins there are.

Teacher focus for activity

Suggestions for facilitating the problem solving process and for developing children's problem solving skills as they work. It includes suggestions for probing questions, discussion points, and areas to look out for.

Less able: Ask children to calculate $\frac{1}{2}$ of 10. Agree that this is how many 50p coins there are.

Optional adult input

Work with the Less able group. Suggest that children model the problem with coins. They may wish to share out half, like sharing half of a pile of sweets. Discuss with them how many are 'half' of the coins.

Plenary

1 Begin with Problem 1 and ask children to explain their solution and how they worked it out. Ask questions such as:
   - *How many 50p coins were there?*
   - *How do you know that?*
   - *How did you work out $\frac{1}{2}$ of 10 coins?*

   Ask a child from the group to total the coins. Encourage them to begin with the largest, and then the next largest, and so on.

2 Repeat this for Problem 2. Ask:
   - *How many coins were 10p? 50p?*
   - *What is the value of the 50p . . . 10p coins?*
   - *How many coins were 5p? How do you know that?*
   - *How did you work out $\frac{1}{4}$ of 12 coins?*

   Again, when children have given their solution ask a child from the group to count out coins to demonstrate how the total was reached.

3 For Problem 3 discuss how many coins were £1 and 50p and how children worked this out. Ask:
   - *How many coins were 5p?*
   - *How do you know that?*
   - *How much are the 5p coins worth?*
   - *How did you calculate $\frac{1}{3}$ of 24 coins?*

   Ask a child to put out the 24 coins and total them, beginning with the £1 coins.

4 Discuss how the fractions refer to the number of the coins, not their value. For Problem 1 ask:
   - *What does 'half' mean in the problem?*
   - *How much are the 50p coins worth?*
   - *Is this the same value as the other 5 coins?*

   Repeat this for the other problems if children are unsure about the meaning of the fractions used in these contexts.

   See **Useful mathematical information** pages 86–87 for more information about finding fractions of quantities.

5 Discuss children's recording. Ask one child from each group to show their working out. Remind the class how ideas or calculations that are crossed out can help them work towards an answer, ensure they don't repeat any possibilities and give them something to check their answer against.

Development

Pose 'what if . . .?' questions if children finish, e.g. *What if half of the coins in his box were 20p coins instead of 50p coins?*

Children could try this problem for homework:

Sarah has 20 coins in her moneybox.
Half of the coins are £2 coins.
A quarter of the coins are 50p.
She also has two £1 coins and a 10p.
The rest are 20p coins.
How much money does she have in total?

Solutions

1 (10 coins)
   If $\frac{1}{2}$ of the coins are 50p coins, then there are five 50p coins.
   So, the total is
   $(5 \times 50p) + £1 + (2 \times 2p) + 5p + 10p$
   $= £2.50 + £1 + 4p + 5p + 10p = $ **£3.69**

2 (12 coins)
   If $\frac{1}{4}$ of the coins are 10p and $\frac{1}{4}$ are 50p then there are three 10p coins and three 50p coins.
   The other 6 coins make up the other half. These are two £1 coins, two £2 coins, and two 5p coins.
   The total is
   $(3 \times 10p) + (3 \times 50p) + (2 \times £1) + (2 \times £2) + (2 \times 5p)$
   $= 30p + £1.50 + £2 + £4 + 10p = $ **£7.90**

3 (24 coins)
   Each third of the coins is eight £1 coins; eight 50p coins; three 20p coins, two 10p coins and three 5p coins.
   The total is
   $(8 \times £1) + (8 \times 50p) + (3 \times 20p) + (2 \times 10p) + (3 \times 5p)$
   $= £8 + £4 + 60p + 20p + 15p = $ **£12.95**

Development solution

(20 coins)
$\frac{1}{2}$ (10) are £2 coins. $\frac{1}{4}$ (5) are 50p and there are two £1 coins, one 10p and two 20p coins.
The total is $(10 \times £2) + (5 \times 50p) + (2 \times £1) + 10p + 40p$
$= £20 + £2.50 + £2 + 50p = $ **£25.00**

61

Lesson structure

Lessons have the recommended 3-part structure, but there is a slightly different emphasis on each part. As it is intended that children solve the problem in their own way, your input at the start of the activity is comparatively brief and is mainly concerned with introducing the problem and checking that children understand what is required.

The main teaching will take place indirectly, through probing questions, hints and suggestions as children work. Direct teaching takes place in the plenary, as solutions, problem solving methods and the mathematics involved are discussed. The plenary therefore contains much greater detail than the problem introduction. It offers opportunities for children to:

- use appropriate vocabulary;
- compare their strategies and solutions;
- listen to explanations, and develop their understanding of mathematical ideas and strategies;
- ask and answer questions.

Differentiation

The problems in this book are differentiated in various ways:

- By level of difficulty.

  Here there are different activities for different ability groups. Early finishers may be able to progress to an activity for a higher ability group.

- By outcome.

  Here children are expected to approach the problem in more or less sophisticated ways, applying mathematical knowledge and understanding at their own level.

- By resource used as support.

  Here children can choose different resources to support them, such as working mentally, using pencil and paper, using an empty number line or using a 100 square. Sometimes a hint may be provided for lower ability groups.

- By level of support.

  Here, especially where additional adults are available, groups can be targeted for specific support.

Questioning techniques

There will be many opportunities to ask questions during a problem solving lesson.

Closed questions will give a response of yes or no, or elicit specific knowledge. They can be used to check understanding. Examples include:

- *Do you understand?* (yes/no)
- *What is half of 100?* (50)

Open questions allow children the opportunity to give a range of responses. Examples include:

- *Which 2 numbers added together would give the answer 50?* (45 + 5; 42 + 8; 25 + 25; 21 + 29 . . .)
- *How could you solve this problem?*

Probing questions are nearly always open in the sense that they require a carefully thought out answer, where children decide how to explain their mathematics. These questions will give you the opportunity to assess their understanding. Examples include:

- *How did you work that out? Is there another way?*
- *What would happen if the numbers were changed to . . .? Would that make a difference? Why is that?*
- *Roughly what answer do you expect to get? How did you come to that estimate?*

Optional adult input

Children may need support and encouragement while they gain familiarity and confidence with working in a new way, or if they have limited experience of solving problems. You may find it helpful, if possible, to arrange for some additional classroom help, particularly when first using this resource.

There are suggestions in each lesson plan as to which group any additional adult could help with and in what way. Here are some general suggestions about how to make best use of an additional adult:

- fully brief them about the problem for that lesson and what your expectations are for each ability group;
- make sure that they understand that children should be allowed to solve a problem in their own way, even if at times it appears that they are going down a blind alley;
- encourage use of suggested probing questions from the **Teacher focus for activity** section of each lesson. Also suggest the following 'catch all' questions:
  - *Can you explain what you have done so far?*
  - *Why did you do that?*
  - *What are you going to do next?*

Class organisation

The lessons in Apex Maths have been specifically designed as whole-class numeracy lessons.

The differentiated ways in which the problems are presented make them ideal for mixed-age classes. They are also highly suitable for schools in which children are set by ability for mathematics lessons. The higher ability sets can work on the main problem and the average and lower ability sets can work on the differentiated presentations of the problem.

In mixed ability classes, children should be broadly grouped in the classroom according to ability. This will facilitate group discussion with the teacher if needed. It will also avoid children 'borrowing' clues or additional directions provided for children of a lesser ability.

Children should ideally work in pairs or 3s when they are working on a problem or investigation. This will stimulate discussion – an essential component of the problem solving process.

Resources

Simple resources will be needed to support these activities, all of which are readily available. Some may be essential to the successful outcome of the activity. Others should be made available, so children can make decisions on resources needed.

General resources that may be useful, include:
- individual whiteboards
- number lines (PCMs 4, 13 and 14)
- 100 square (PCM 5)
- digit cards (PCM 7)
- calculators
- overhead projector calculator
- counters and centimetre cubes
- interlocking cubes
- rods such as Cuisenaire, or straws
- squared and dotty paper (centimetre squares)
- measuring tapes.

Calculators

Some problem solving or investigatory procedures might involve many tedious or repetitive calculations that do not develop children's mathematical understanding. Others might involve calculations which are just beyond the ability of children, who otherwise are making excellent progress towards solving the problem. In these cases teachers should use their discretion as to whether to allow some children to use a calculator. In lessons in which this situation is likely to occur calculators are listed with the resources to be made available.

Assessment

While children are working at the problem, and during the plenary, target pairs and individuals in order to assess their skills in problem solving. Use probing questions, such as the examples given under **Questioning techniques** (page 10), and those given within the teacher's notes for the lesson. By targeting specific children during each problem solving lesson it is possible to ensure that all children will be assessed through discussion over time.

Look for signs of consistency in approach to a given problem. Make sure that children read all of the data and are able to sort which data is relevant and which should be discarded.

When discussing their work, take the opportunity to identify whether children have understood the mathematics involved. This is an ideal time to check whether there are any misconceptions that need remedying.

Watch for children who rely too heavily upon their partner for:
- **how to solve the problem:** Does the child understand what the problem involves?
- **mathematical calculations:** Does the child understand which calculation strategies and procedures to use, and can they use these themselves?
- **recording the problem:** Is the child able to suggest how the results might be presented?
- **answering open and probing questions and reporting back in the plenary:** Is the child able to articulate their thinking? Does the child have the appropriate vocabulary and can they use it appropriately to express mathematical ideas and explanations? Are they given enough response time?

During the problem solving lesson take time to stand back and observe what the children are doing.
- Do children cooperate?
- Are they working collaboratively?
- Do they both contribute to the discussion, or does one dominate, taking the lead?
- Do they use appropriate mathematical language in order to express their ideas?

Scope and sequence chart

This chart lists all the problems together with:

- the problem solving objectives addressed (from the *NNS Framework for teaching mathematics*);
- the likely outcome levels for each ability group for Attainment Target 1 (Using and Applying Maths) in the *National Curriculum for England: Mathematics;*
- the *Framework* topics addressed by each problem.

Because children will solve problems in different ways, using different aspect of mathematics, the specific *Framework* objectives that will be addressed will vary. For this reason, only the topics that are likely to be addressed have been referenced.

* Indicates that the general mathematical content may extend the most able beyond the Year 3 objectives in the *Framework for teaching mathematics.*

Problem	Choose and use appropriate operations and ways of calculating	Explain methods and reasoning, orally and, where appropriate, in writing	Solve mathematical problems or puzzles, recognise simple patterns or relationships ... Suggest extensions by asking 'What if...?' or 'What could I try next?'	Investigate a general statement about familiar numbers or shapes by finding examples that satisfy it.	Solve word problems involving numbers in 'real life' ... using 1 or 2 steps. Explain how the problem was solved	Ma1 Using and applying mathematics Level/outcome — More able	Average	Less able	Mathematical topics
1 Our milkman*	■	■	■			Level 3/4	Level 3	Level 2	Number sequences
2 Palindromes*	■	■	■			Level 3	Level 2/3	Level 2	Place value
3 The mysterious dungeon*	■	■	■			Level 3	Level 2/3	Level 2	Place value; Mental calculation strategies
4 The skipping rope*	■	■	■			Level 3	Level 2/3	Level 2	Fractions; Length
5 The fruit bowl*	■	■	■			Level 3	Level 2/3	Level 2	Fractions of numbers
6 Close to one hundred	■	■	■			Level 3	Level 2/3	Level 2	Place value; Length
7 Which way round?	■	■	■	■		Level 3	Level 2/3	Level 2	Place value; Addition
8 Largest and smallest totals*	■	■	■	■		Level 3	Level 2/3	Level 2	Addition
9 Total thirty-one	■	■	■	■		Level 3	Level 2/3	Level 2	Addition
10 Telephone numbers*	■	■	■			Level 3	Level 2/3	Level 2	Addition
11 Make a number*	■	■	■			Level 3	Level 2/3	Level 2	Addition; Subtraction
12 Shoes, dogs and cats*	■	■	■			Level 3	Level 2/3	Level 2	Addition; Subtraction

Problem	Problem solving objectives involved					MA1 Using and applying mathematics Level/outcome			Mathematical topics
						More able	Average	Less able	
13 Count down to zero*	■	■	■	■		Level 3	Level 2/3	Level 2	Subtraction
14 Four in a row	■	■	■			Level 3/4	Level 2/3	Level 2	Multiplication; Mental calculations
15 A pocketful of money	■	■	■		■	Level 3	Level 2/3	Level 2	Addition; Money
16 Mystery numbers	■	■	■			Level 3	Level 2/3	Level 2	Multiplication; Division
17 Calculator magic*	■	■	■			Level 3	Level 2/3	Level 2	Addition; Mental calculation strategies $(+ - \times \div)$
18 A street scene*	■	■	■			Level 3	Level 2/3	Level 2	Multiplication; Doubling
19 The blacksmith	■	■	■			Level 3	Level 2/3	Level 2	Multiplication; Doubling
20 Money box	■	■	■			Level 3	Level 2/3	Level 2	Fractions; Money; Addition; Multiplication
21 Ice cream cones	■	■	■			Level 3	Level 2/3	Level 2	Handling data: sorting by tables
22 Pick up sticks	■	■	■			Level 3	Level 2/3	Level 2	Counting; Estimating
23 Sticky squares	■	■	■			Level 3	Level 2/3	Level 2	Counting
24 Squares and triangles		■	■			Level 3	Level 2/3	Level 2	Shape and space
25 Fold a shape			■	■		Level 3	Level 2/3	Level 2	Shape and space
26 Make that shape			■			Level 3	Level 2/3	Level 2	Shape and space
27 Jamie's walk			■			Level 3	Level 2/3	Level 2	Position, direction and movement
28 A weighty problem*	■	■	■		■	Level 3/4	Level 2/3	Level 2	Weight; Estimating; Addition; Multiplication
29 Tennis matches		■	■		■	Level 3	Level 2/3	Level 2	Time; Handling data
30 Going to the cinema		■	■		■	Level 3	Level 2/3	Level 2	Time; Handling data

Scotland 5–14 Guidelines

		Problem solving and enquiry	Information handling	Range and type of numbers	Money	Add and subtract	Multiply and divide	Fractions, percentages and ratio	Patterns and sequences	Functions and equations	Measure and estimate	Time	Shape, position and movement
1	Our milkman	●	●				●		●				
2	Palindromes	●		●					●				
3	The mysterious dungeon	●	●			●	●						
4	The skipping rope	●	●	●			●	●					
5	The fruit bowl	●	●	●			●	●					
6	Close to one hundred	●				●							
7	Which way round?	●				●							
8	Largest and smallest totals	●				●				●			
9	Total thirty-one	●				●			●				
10	Telephone numbers	●				●			●				
11	Make a number	●				●				●			
12	Shoes, dogs and cats	●	●				●						
13	Count down to zero	●		●		●							
14	Four in a row	●		●			●			●			
15	A pocketful of money	●	●		●	●							
16	Mystery numbers	●					●			●			
17	Calculator magic	●				●	●			●			
18	A street scene	●	●				●						
19	The blacksmith	●			●	●	●		●				
20	Money box	●			●	●	●	●					
21	Ice cream cones	●	●						●				
22	Pick up sticks	●				●			●				
23	Sticky squares	●				●			●				
24	Squares and triangles	●											●
25	Fold a shape	●											●
26	Make that shape	●											●
27	Jamie's walk	●											●
28	A weighty problem	●				●	●				●		
29	Tennis matches	●	●									●	
30	Going to the cinema	●	●									●	

In each activity, children will need to employ the three problem-solving steps of (1) starting, (2) doing and (3) reporting on a task. Encourage children to choose appropriate strategies at each stage, and to evaluate their choices.

Northern Ireland Lines of Development (Levels 2 and 3)

'Processes in mathematics' applies to all lessons.

	Lesson	Related Lines of Development
1	Our milkman	N2.27, N3.12
2	Palindromes	N2.11, N2.13, R3.4
3	The mysterious dungeon	N2.6, N2.8, N2.9, N2.13, N2.27, N3.12, N3.17
4	The skipping rope	N3.17, N3.20
5	The fruit bowl	N2.30, N3.16, N3.17
6	Close to one hundred	N2.16, N2.19, N2.20, N3.4
7	Which way round?	N2.11, N2.16, N2.19, N2.20
8	Largest and smallest totals	N2.11, N2.16, N2.20, N3.5
9	Total thirty-one	N2.4, N2.19
10	Telephone numbers	N2.4, N2.11, N2.19, N3.4
11	Make a number	N2.2, N2.9, N2.18, N2.21, N2.24, N3.3
12	Shoes, dogs and cats	N2.2, N2.8, HD2.2, HD2.3
13	Count down to zero	N2.5, N2.8, N3.3
14	Four in a row	N3.10, N3.11, N3.12, N3.14
15	A pocketful of money	N2.15, N2.32, N3.8
16	Mystery numbers	N3.17, N3.20, N3.22, N3.23
17	Calculator magic	N2.20, N2.21, N3.12, N3.14, N3.17, N3.23, R3.5
18	A street scene	N3.10, N3.11, N3.12, R3.5
19	The blacksmith	N2.27, N3.6, N3.14, N3.15, R3.3
20	Money box	N2.28, N2.32, N3.15, N3.16, N3.17
21	Ice cream cones	HD2.1, HD2.2, HD2.3, HD2.4, HD3.4
22	Pick up sticks	N2.4, N2.14, N3.10, R2.3, R2.4
23	Sticky squares	N2.6, N2.14, N3.10, R2.3, R2.4
24	Squares and triangles	S2.3, SP3.1, SP3.2, SP3.3, SP3.4
25	Fold a shape	S2.3, S3.2, S3.10
26	Make that shape	A3.1, S3.6, SP3.3, SP3.4
27	Jamie's walk	SP2.1, SP2.2, SP3.4, SP3.6
28	A weighty problem	M3.1, M3.2, M3.5
29	Tennis matches	T2.3, HD2.4, HD3.1, HD3.4
30	Going to the cinema	T2.3, T2.4, T3.2, T3.6, HD2.4, HD3.1, HD3.4

Oral and mental problem solving starters

Oral and mental activities for the start of each lesson can be selected from this bank of problem solving starters or from other sources.

Children could show their answers using digit cards or fans, individual whiteboards or scraps of paper. This allows less confident children to attempt answers without fear of being incorrect in front of others. It also enables you to survey all children's answers, making a note of common errors or responses from particular individuals.

Allow children time to think about a problem before you expect an answer. You could ask them to wait for a signal from you before they show their answers. This allows all children an equal opportunity to answer questions, not just the quicker or more confident ones.

Resources which will be useful for these activities include: large teaching numerals, yarn/string and scissors, overhead projector and OHP calculator, centimetre-squared paper, shape tiles, clock faces.

1 Odds and evens

(counting; number sequences)

Invite children to count with you, in 2s, starting from any 2-digit number, to at least 100 and back again. Ask:

- *Were the numbers that we said odd or even?*
- *How do you know that?*
- *What is the next number in the counting pattern: 65, 67, 69?*

Repeat this for other starting numbers.

2 What am I?

(properties of numbers)

This is a game where you give some information about a number and children try to work out what the number is. Children would benefit from using small whiteboards and pens, so that they can write down their answers to show you.

For the number 842 say:

- *I have 3 digits.*
- *My middle digit is twice the smallest value digit and half the biggest value digit.*
- *What number am I?*

And for the number 971:

- *I have more than 2 and fewer than 4 digits.*
- *All my digits are odd.*
- *My middle digit is 6 larger than my smallest value digit.*
- *My digit in the largest place is the largest digit you can have, and is 2 more than my middle digit.*
- *What number am I?*

3 Place value riddles

(place value)

Explain that you will give some information about the place value of 3 digits and would like children to write down the number that they think the digits make. Write the 3 digits on the board. If children have whiteboards and pens they can write down their answers to show you. For 1, 2, 3 and the number 312, say:

- *The largest digit is in the greatest value place.*
- *The smallest digit is in the middle.*
- *What is my number? Show me.*

For the digits 258 and the number 528, say:

- *The digit in the smallest place is the largest.*
- *My largest value place has an odd digit.*
- *What is my number? Show me.*

This can be extended to include 4-digit numbers.

4 Fraction snap

(equivalent fractions)

Explain that you will say a fraction. Ask children to think of a fraction that is the same value and to write it on their whiteboards. When you say 'Show me', children hold up their boards.

For example:

You say	Children write
One half	$\frac{2}{4}, \frac{3}{6}, \frac{4}{8}, \frac{5}{10} \cdots$
One third	$\frac{2}{6}, \frac{4}{12}$
Two quarters	$\frac{1}{2}, \frac{3}{6}, \frac{4}{8} \cdots$
One fifth	$\frac{2}{10}$

Discuss all the possible answers and why they are the same. Ask children to show each other their equivalents first, before the teacher.

5 Wholes

(add or subtract fractions to make 1)

Explain that you will say a fraction, and you would like children to write down on their whiteboards what should be added to the fraction to make 1. Fractions could include: $\frac{1}{2}, \frac{1}{4}, \frac{3}{4}, \frac{1}{3}, \frac{2}{3}, \frac{1}{5}, \frac{3}{5}, \frac{1}{6}, \frac{1}{8} \cdots$

Ask questions such as:

- *How do you know that $\frac{1}{4}$ and $\frac{3}{4}$ makes 1?*
- *How did you work it out?*
- *Who worked this out a different way?*

6 One hundred

(rapid recall of addition and subtraction facts)

Explain that you will say a multiple of 5 and you would like children to write down the other number to total 100 on their whiteboards. When you say 'Show me' children hold up their boards for you to see their responses. So, if you say '35', the children should write down 65. Ask questions such as:

- *How did you work that out?*
- *What if, instead of 35, I had said 36? What number would you need to write down then?*
- *How do you know that?*
- *How do you know if a number is a multiple of 5? (The units digit will always be '5' or '0'.)*

7 Make a calculation

(mental calculation strategies)

Ask children to sit in a circle. Explain that you will start by saying a calculation. The first child in the circle says the answer, and then uses that answer as the start of the next calculation. Decide whether to put a ceiling on the size of numbers used, such as up to 30, up to 50 . . . Children can use addition or subtraction for this. When everyone has had a turn, provide opportunities for children to evaluate their work. Ask:

- *What did you find easy/hard about that activity?*
- *How did you decide what sort of calculation to say?*
- *Is it easier to add or subtract? Why? (You may like to reinforce the link between addition and subtraction with this question.)*

8 Card pick

(know what each digit represents)

You will need some large digit cards, 1–9, and a box or bag. Tell children that in the box/bag are some digit cards. Explain that you will choose 2 cards at random. On their whiteboards children write down the 2 possible numbers that they can make with the digits. If you show them 2 and 5, they can write down 25 and 52.

When children are confident about what to do, repeat the activity with 3 cards. Ask questions such as:

- *How do you know that is the largest possible number?*
- For the cards '1', '6', '9': *How do you know that 961 is the largest number?*
- *For the largest/smallest number, which digit needs to be in the hundreds/tens/units? Why?*

9 Count on

(counting in 2s, 3s, and 6s)

Begin with counting on in 2s or 3s. Explain that the count will begin from zero, and ask children to say the next number, keeping a good pace. When this has 'warmed them up', make it more difficult, by asking them to count in 6s, in the same way. Now the pace may be slower, but do not let it dawdle. When children have counted to 100 in this way, ask:

- *How did you work out the next number?*
- *What is the link between counting in 2s, counting in 3s, and counting in 6s?*
- *Suppose we counted in 12s. What links would there be?*

This activity encourages children to make links between the 2, 3 and 6 times tables.

10 Bingo!

(mental calculation strategies; rapid recall of addition and subtraction facts)

Ask children to draw a 3 × 3 grid on their whiteboards, and to write a number between 1 and 50 in each square. Encourage children to do this without consulting their neighbours. Explain that you will say some calculations. If they have the answer they put a cross through that number. The winner is the first person to cross through 3 numbers in a row, column or diagonal. Make a note of the questions/answers you have called out, so that you can check if children have been recording accurately when someone shouts 'Bingo'.

Ask addition and subtraction questions, such as:

- *What is the sum of 14, 15 and 16?* (45)
- *How many fewer is 13 than 29?* (16)
- *What is the difference between 50 and 11?* (39)

Play the game once. Now, invite children to make a new 3 × 3 grid, and play the game again. Ask:

- *How did you choose your numbers? Why did you make that choice?*

Talk about how, in a game like this, it is not possible to 'guess' what the numbers in the grid should be.

11 Show me number properties

(properties of numbers)

Provide each child with a set of 0–9 digit cards or a number fan. Explain that you will say a property of a number, and would like children to hold up a number that fits that property. Say, for example:

- *A number between 50 and 60 that is odd.*
- *An even number less than 100 but more than 95.*
- *An odd number greater than 200.*
- *A number that is a multiple of 5.*
- *A number that can be divided by 10.*

When children show you, discuss the different possible outcomes, so that children realise there may be more than one answer.

12 What matters?

(problems involving 'real life', money and measures)

Explain that you will tell a story. Ask the children to listen carefully and work out the answer to the question. The story should contain surplus information which is not relevant to the mathematics. For example:

- *Josh and Sam walked along the path and noticed that all the cars that were parked in the road had a '2' on their number plate. Josh counted the cars and said to Sam 'If I multiply the number of cars by 3 and add 5 the answer is 20.' How many cars were there?* (5)
- *Jen and Karis were wearing their PE kit, and had just completed some giant steps around the hall. They noticed that all the hoops had been given out in PE and there were not enough for them to have any. Jen said 'If I add the number of boys with hoops to the number of girls*

with hoops that makes 30.' Karis said 'If we had hoops as well, then there would be 16 girls with hoops'. Can you work out how many boys had hoops? (16).

Discuss each problem. Ask children how they worked out the answer. Also ask which information they could ignore, and why.

13 Count back

(counting back in 2s, 3s and 6s)

Ask children to sit in a circle. Starting at 100 they take turns to count back in 2s. Repeat this for counting back in 3s. Now ask the children to count back in 6s. Ask:

- *How did you work out the next number?*
- *Can 100 be divided exactly by 2/3/6? How do you know that?*

14 Thirty-six

(rapid recall of multiplication facts)

Explain that the answer to the multiplication is 36. Invite children to think what the multiplication could be. Allow them to share possible answers in pairs. Ask various children to write their multiplication sentence on the board. Answers could include:
$2 \times 18, 3 \times 12, 4 \times 9, 6 \times 6, 9 \times 4, 12 \times 3, 18 \times 2$
You may wish to discuss whether, e.g. 2×18 is the same as 18×2.
Repeat this for different starting numbers, such as 24, 48, 30 . . .

15 Estimating lengths

(give a sensible estimate; measure and compare using standard units)

Children will need about 2 m of yarn or string and scissors. Explain that you will say a length and would like them to estimate this, cutting off a length of yarn that they think is approximately that length. Invite children to compare their lengths with others, then measure it. Repeat this a number of times so that they can use their checked estimates to become more accurate. Lengths could include:

- 1 m.
- Half or quarter of a metre.
- 30 cm.
- 2 cm.

Discuss how they may have used actual lengths of string or lengths of feet/arms/objects to help their estimating.

16 What is my number?

(properties of numbers; recall of +, −, × or ÷ facts)

Explain that you will say some number facts and would like children to work out what number you are thinking of.

For 15:

- *My number is a multiple of both 5 and 3.*
- *It can't be divided by 2.*
- *It is less than 20.*
- *What is my number?*

For 18:

- *My number is less than 20.*
- *It is divisible by 2 and 3.*
- *It is also a multiple of 6.*
- *What is my number?*

Repeat this for other numbers. Encourage children to explain how they worked out the number.

17 Calculator patterns

(number sequences; understanding + and −)

You will need the overhead projector and OHP calculator. If you do not have an OHP calculator, use a normal one, and allow children to follow on their own calculator. Set the calculator to add a given number repeatedly:

5 + + =

This sets the constant function to add 5. Decide upon the starting number, such as 24. Put 24 into the display and ask children to watch as you press = = =. The display should read 29, 34, 39. Ask:

- *What is the pattern?*
- *What do you think the next number will be? And the next?*

Press = = to show children that they were correct.

Re-set the display by pressing AC or C twice, then input another constant function, deciding whether to use + + =, or − − = for a subtraction pattern.

18 Follow my leader

(mental calculation strategies; rapid recall of +, −, × or ÷ facts)

Explain that children will listen carefully to some instructions, beginning with a given number. Children should work mentally to find the answer and write this on their whiteboards. When you say 'Show me' they hold up their boards.

For example:

- *Start with 27; add 9; divide by 3. What number do you have now?* (12)
- *Start with 14; double it; subtract 3; divide by 5. What number do you have?* (5)

Invite children to explain the strategies that they used to solve this. Repeat using a different starting number and operations.

You could use a combination of operations, as above, or focus on those that need development.

19 Double, halve or add or subtract one

(doubling or halving; mental calculation strategies)

This is a game for the whole class to play, taking turns around the class to give a response. Explain that you will begin by saying a number sentence to which the first child gives the answer. That child uses the answer to begin their number sentence. Each number sentence should involve doubling or halving, adding or subtracting 1. For example, the sequence could begin:

- Double 15.
- 30 subtract 1.
- Double 29 . . .

Set some boundaries if necessary, such as: *no answer larger than . . .*

20 Money fractions

(fractions of numbers)

Use number fans or whiteboards. Ask children to work out some simple fractions of money.

- *What is $\frac{1}{2}$, $\frac{1}{4}$, $\frac{1}{5}$ of 40 pence . . . 80 pence?*
- *What is $\frac{1}{2}$, $\frac{1}{4}$, $\frac{1}{5}$ of £1?*
- *If I take $\frac{1}{4}$ of £1 away how much do I have left? What fraction is that?*
- *John has 60 pence in his pocket. He spends $\frac{1}{3}$ of it on sweets. How much does he have left?*

Discuss children's methods, such as finding $\frac{1}{4}$ by halving and halving again.

Repeat for other amounts. Encourage children to explain the strategies that they used.

21 Make a total

(mental calculation strategies)

Write some numbers on the board, such as: 26, 18, 35, 14, 37. Ask questions such as:

- *Tell me 2 numbers that would give an even total. How do you know that?*
- *And 2 that would give an odd total?*
- *2 numbers whose total has a 9 in the units?*
- *2 numbers whose total has a 7 in the tens?*
- *How did you work that out?*

Discuss strategies that children use in adding such as partitioning, bridging through tens, known number facts. Discuss which they prefer and why.

This can be repeated with other starting numbers.

22 What comes next?

(number sequences)

Begin by writing 3 numbers on the board that are part of a number sequence, such as: 16, 21, 26. Ask *What comes next?* Ask children to explain how they worked this out, then repeat for other sequences of numbers, including sequences that count down, such as: 4, 8, 12; 12, 15, 18; 30, 26, 22.

23 Fizz buzz for multiples of 3, 4 and 12

(rapid recall of multiplication facts)

Explain that you would like children to count around the class, starting from zero. Every time the number is a multiple of 3, they say 'fizz' and if it is a multiple of 4 they say 'buzz'. Of course, if the number is a multiple of 3 or 4, that is, a multiple of 12, they say 'fizz buzz'.

Stop every so often, and ask a child to explain why they said, 'fizz', 'buzz' or 'fizz buzz'.

24 Imagine it!

(shape and space)

Provide children with whiteboards and pens. Explain that children will shut their eyes and listen carefully to some sentences about shapes. Ask them to imagine in their heads what you say:

- *Draw a square in your head;*
- *Now cut it in half moving from the bottom left corner to the top right corner;*
- *Draw the new shapes that you have made on your whiteboard.*

Or:

- *Begin with a right-angled triangle.*
- *Now take another right-angled triangle. Turn this one until you can put the 2 triangles together to make an even larger triangle.*
- *Draw your new shape.*

Let children show you and discuss how they imagined their shape. Allow some to draw on the board while you repeat a description. Promote discussion and repeat this for other shapes.

25 Draw me

(properties of 2-D shapes)

Provide children with whiteboards and pens and ask children to listen carefully to the description of a shape that they then draw. They can hold up the boards when you say '*Show me*' so that their responses can be checked. Say:

- *I have 4 sides equal in length and 4 right angles.* (Square)
- *I have 3 sides and a right angle.* (Right-angled triangle)
- *I am a pentagon with all my sides the same length.* (5 equal sides)

Repeat this for other shapes such as: rectangle, star, hexagon, octagon or semi-circle.

26 Shape sort

(classify 2-D shapes)

On each table provide some shape tiles including squares, rectangles, right-angled triangles, other triangles, pentagons, hexagons, octagons, circles, semi-circles . . . Explain that you are thinking of a shape, and that you will say some of the properties of the shape. Ask children to sort the shape tiles after each property, getting rid of those that do not fit. Each pair of children should work together for this activity. Expect children to discuss what they are doing, but keep a sharp pace, as well. For a pentagon you might say:

- *My shape has no curves.*
- *It has straight edges that are all the same length.*
- *My shape has 5 vertices.*

Repeat for other shapes.

27 Turtle moves

(position, direction and movement)

Provide children with a sheet of centimetre-squared paper, and ask them to carefully mark out a square with sides of 5 squares each. They label the corners like this:

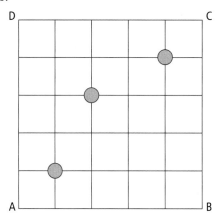

Ask children to put 3 small pencil circles onto their grids to mark where they think treasure might be buried. These circles must be where 2 lines on the grid cross. Now give instructions for moving around the grid and ask children to mark the route with their pencils:

- *Start at A facing towards D. Forward 3.*
- *Turn right.*
- *Forward 4.*
- *Turn left.*
- *Forward 1.*
- *Has anyone buried treasure here? Score a point if you have.*

As you develop this activity introduce other vocabulary of position and direction, e.g. N, S, E, W, clockwise, anti-clockwise and quarter turn.

Using an enlarged version of the grid, check the moves with children, then repeat this with different forward/backward and turn moves.

28 A heavy load

(problems involving 'real life', money or measures)

Explain that you will say some weight word problems and would like children to work out the answers. Begin with a simple problem, and then provide stories where there is a lot of data to sift to work out what is needed:

- *Milly weighs her school bag and finds that it is twice as heavy as a box of cornflakes that weighs 500 grams. How heavy is her school bag?* (1 kilogram)

- *Jack and his mum take the cat to the vet. The vet gives them some medicine but explains that they will need to weigh the cat to work out how much medicine it needs. The medicine packet reads 'cats up to 4 kilograms in weight have 1 tablet, and heavier cats have 2 tablets'. Jack holds the cat and stands on the scales. The reading is 30 kilograms. Then Jack alone stands on the scales. The reading is 27 kilograms. How many tablets does the cat need?* (1 tablet: the cat weighs 3 kilograms.)

Invite children to explain the strategies that they used to find the solution.

29 Clock times

(read times to 5 minutes on analogue/digital clocks)

Provide clock faces. Explain that you will say a time, and ask children to set the clocks to the time that you say. Use both analogue and digital language:

- *Quarter to 5.*
- *7:35.*
- *20 past 3 in the afternoon (pm).*
- *10 to midnight.*

Reinforce how, e.g. '7:35' is 35 minutes 'past' 7 or 25 minutes 'to' 8.

30 Time problems

(problems involving 'real life', money or measures)

Explain that you will ask some time word problems. Ask children to work out the answers and invite some of them to explain the strategies that they used.

- *I need to be at work by 8:15 am. The journey takes 20 minutes by car. What time must I leave home?* (7:55 or 5 to 8)
- *The cake went in the oven at 10:15 and came out at 10:40. How long was it in the oven?* (25 minutes)

If children cope well with these, move on to more challenging examples such as:

- *The buses leave the station every 30 minutes, starting at 10 minutes past the hour. My train gets in at half past 6. Which bus will I catch?* (6:40 or 20 to 7)
- *The journey by aeroplane takes $3\frac{1}{2}$ hours. The plane leaves the airport at 11:40 pm on Tuesday. What day and time will the plane arrive?* (Wednesday, 3:10 am or 10 past 3 in the morning)

1 Our milkman

Minimum prior experience

odd and even numbers

Resources

Textbook pages 4 and 5, PCM 1, squared paper, plain paper, counters, (milk crate / box with dividers, bottles/balls)

Key vocabulary

odd, even, arrange, rearrange, change over, investigate, row, column, diagonal

What's the problem?

There are 12 bottles of milk to arrange in a milk crate so that each row and column has an even number of bottles. The milk crate is in a 4 × 4 arrangement.

Problem solving objectives

- Choose and use appropriate number operations and appropriate ways of calculating (mental, mental with jottings, pencil and paper) to solve problems.
- Explain methods and reasoning orally and, where appropriate, in writing.
- Solve mathematical problems or puzzles, recognise simple patterns and relationships, generalise and predict. Suggest extensions by asking 'What if . . .?'

Differentiation

The activity on Textbook pages 4 and 5 is for the whole class, with differentiation by outcome.

Introducing the problem

If a milk crate or box with dividers is available, show children the view looking down on it. With a few bottles or balls placed in, they will understand how it appears as a bird's eye view in the book.

Ask children to look at the picture of the milk crate on their Textbook page. It is possible that children may not have seen a milk crate.

Explain the problem. *The grid on the page represents the spaces in the milk crate. Your task is to find a way to place the bottles into the crate so that each row and each column has an even number of bottles.*

Reinforce what an even number is and ask children for examples to check their understanding.

Ask children to decide how they will record what they have done. They can use PCM 1 if they wish. Ask children to write a few sentences to explain their method, and how they found their solution.

Teacher focus for activity

All children: It is better if children model the problem using the counters. If they move straight away to recording on paper, then crossings out and erasures can result in fewer than 12 bottles being recorded.

More able and Average: Challenge children to find as many possible solutions as they can. Once they have found 1 solution, then suggest that they use that to find others.

Less able: Ask children to explain what they have to do, and check that they understand what odd and even means, asking, for example: *Which rows/columns have an even/odd number of spaces?*

As children work, ask questions such as:

- *Can you explain to me what the problem is about?*
- *What have you tried so far? What have you learnt?*
- *What could you try next? Why do you think that will help you?*

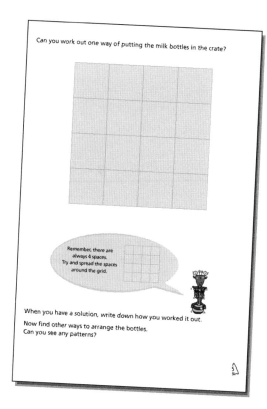

Optional adult input

Work with the Average group. Challenge children, in the time available, to find a number of different solutions.

Plenary

1 Draw a large 4 × 4 grid on the board and invite various children to draw in a solution.

For each solution ask:

- *Does each row and column have an even number of bottles?*

- *Is this a different solution from the others that we have?*

2 Ask children to check each solution carefully, making sure that each one is unique. Children may, for example, have a mirror image of a previous solution. Where solutions are mirror images of each other, discuss whether the solutions are the same or different, and invite children to explain their thinking carefully.

The key is to always have 2 rows of 4 and 2 columns of 2, or vice versa wherever you put the counters.

3 When a number of solutions have been identified, discuss how children set about the task. Responses may include:

- random placement of counters;

- began randomly, but then began to understand the problem more clearly, so looked for a way of placing the counters in even quantities;

- looked at the odd/even number of spaces;

- looked at the location of spaces on the board;

- rearrange the bottles in columns of 4 to give further solutions;

- realised there must be 4 spaces in total, so rearranged bottles trying to have an even number in rows/columns.

If there are 3 columns (or rows) of 4, then you end up with an odd total in each row. Many children will think of this as a possible solution without actually checking both columns and rows (see diagram).

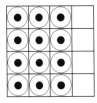

Example of incorrect solution

Children can use the notes that they made to help them to answer how they went about solving the problem.

The mathematics in this problem is fairly straightforward. It is the strategies that the children adopt and the thinking behind these that is important, so allow plenty of time for discussing these.

Development

Decide whether to compile a collection of the solutions and mount a wall display of these for children to study. This may lead to further solutions being found which children can record on blank copies of PCM 1.

Solutions

These are 2 possible solutions.

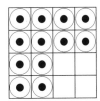

Other solutions are likely to be a rearrangement of this. See **Useful mathematical information**, page 82 for some more solutions.

2 Palindromes

Minimum prior experience

ThHTU numbers for More able; HTU numbers for Average and Less able

Resources

Textbook page 6, paper for recording

Key vocabulary

units, ones, tens, hundreds, thousands, digit, place, place value, stands for, predict

What's the problem?

Children identify palindromic numbers for a specified number range, explain their methods and predict other solutions through generalisations.

Problem solving objectives

- Choose and use appropriate number operations and appropriate ways of calculating (mental, mental with jottings, pencil and paper) to solve problems.
- Explain methods and reasoning orally and, where appropriate, in writing.
- Solve mathematical problems or puzzles, recognise simple patterns and relationships, generalise and predict. Suggest extensions by asking 'What if . . .?'

Differentiation

The problem on Textbook page 6 is differentiated as follows:

More able: Problem 3: ThHTU.

Average: Problem 1 then 2: HTU between 100 and 500, then 500 and 1000.

Less able: Problem 1: HTU between 100 and 500.

Introducing the problem

Explain what a palindrome is, beginning with palindromic words, such as: did, noon, Mum, level, Hannah . . .

Discuss with children how, if a word is a palindrome, then it reads the same when it is written left to right, as when it is written right to left.

Introduce the idea of palindromic numbers, writing 101 on the board. Invite children to suggest another palindromic number.

Ask children to look at the task in their Textbooks. Check that children look at their group's problem.

Explain that you will be very interested in how they solve the problem. Invite children to decide how they will start the task with their partner, and begin straight away.

Teacher focus for activity

All children: Check that children can identify numbers that are palindromes and explain what is special about them.

More able: If necessary, suggest that children make a list of all the palindromes between 1000 and 1999, then do the same for 2000 to 2999. Ask them what they notice and if they can now work out how many palindromes there are between 3000 and 3999.

Average and Less able: If necessary, suggest that children make a list of all the palindromes between 100 and 199, then do the same for 200 to 299. Ask what they notice and if they can now work out how many palindromes there are between 300 and 399.

As children work, ask questions such as:

- *What have you found out so far?*
- *What will you try next?*
- *Can you spot a pattern? What is it? How does that help you?*

Optional adult input

Work with the Less able group. Check that they can read the numbers that they write, and know the place value of each digit. Be aware of any children who predict numbers and spot patterns.

Plenary

1 Begin with problem 1. Invite the More able group to join in, as they will soon spot how similar the pattern is to theirs.

Ask:

- *Which numbers that are palindromes did you find between 100 and 200?*
- *How many were there? (10)*
- *So, how many do you think there will be between 200 and 300?*

2 Ask children to say the palindromic numbers. If they have understood what is happening, some should be able to do this without looking at their notes.

3 Choose children to write their palindromic numbers on the board. Encourage comments and predictions from children watching, as they write.

4 Now, repeat this for Problem 3, and invite other children to see if they, too, can spot the pattern. Check that children understand the digit place value for thousands, hundreds, tens and units.

Ask for examples of how children recorded their work. Talk about recording systematically, such as making an ordered list, or writing the numbers in a table. Invite children to explain why this is a good method.

They may say that it:

- helps to ensure that no numbers are missed;
- is possible to see a pattern, such as the increase by one each time from zero in the tens (numbers 100 to 1000) and the increase from zero by 1 each time in the tens and hundreds (numbers 1000 to 10 000).

Solutions

1 and 2 A regular pattern emerges when searching for palindromes between 100 and 1000.

101	202	303	404	505	606	707	808	909
111	212	313	414	515	616	717	818	919
121	222	323	424	525	626	727	828	929
131	232	333	434	535	636	737	838	939
141	242	343	444	545	646	747	848	949
151	252	353	454	555	656	757	858	959
161	262	363	464	565	666	767	868	969
171	272	373	474	575	676	777	878	979
181	282	383	484	585	686	787	888	989
191	292	393	494	595	696	797	898	999

For each column, there are 10 rows, so that in each hundred there are 10 palindromic numbers.

There are 90 palindromic numbers between 100 and 1000.

3 Similarly a regular pattern emerges when searching for palindromes between 1000 and 10 000.

1001	2002	3003	4004	5005	6006	7007	8008	9009
1111	2112	3113	4114	5115	6116	7117	8118	9119
1221	2222	3223	4224	5225	6226	7227	8228	9229
1331	2332	3333	4334	5335	6336	7337	8338	9339
1441	2442	3443	4444	5445	6446	7447	8448	9449
1551	2552	3553	4554	5555	6556	7557	8558	9559
1661	2662	3663	4664	5665	6666	7667	8668	9669
1771	2772	3773	4774	5775	6776	7777	8778	9779
1881	2882	3883	4884	5885	6886	7887	8888	9889
1991	2992	3993	4994	5995	6996	7997	8998	9999

For each column, there are 10 rows, so that in each thousand there are 10 palindromic numbers.

There are 90 palindromic numbers between 1000 and 10 000. See **Useful mathematical information**, page 82 for further discussion on palindromes.

3 The mysterious dungeon

3 The mysterious dungeon

A wicked dragon has locked 3 knights in a dungeon. They can escape if they know the secret password. Help them to work out the password.

You have 4 number riddles to solve. They are a, b, c and d below.

Each riddle makes a 2-digit number.

Work out each digit of the number. Write it down.

❶ a The tens digit is 9 minus 6.
The units digit is 4 doubled.

b The tens digit is 5 more than 4.
The units digit is 1 less than 4.

c Multiply 3 by 3.
That gives you the tens digit.
The units digit is not 4 but is in the 4 times table.

d Find the number of months in a year. Now take away the number of days in a week. That gives you the tens digit. Multiply 3 by 2. Add 2. Write your answer in the units place.

Write down each number.
Turn to page 10 to work out the password.

Minimum prior experience

place value; properties of numbers

Resources

Textbook pages 7, 8, 9 and 10, PCM 2, Place value chart (PCM 3), paper, 0–9 digit cards (PCM 7)

Key vocabulary

units, ones, tens, hundreds, thousands, digit, numeral, place, place value, puzzle, add, sum, total

What's the problem?

There are 4 riddles to solve using the 4 operations to calculate individual digits. Some of the information in the riddles is redundant. Children find the digital root of their answers by adding digits, and use a code to find the solution to the problem.

Problem solving objectives

- Choose and use appropriate number operations and appropriate ways of calculating (mental, mental with jottings, pencil and paper) to solve problems.
- Explain methods and reasoning orally and, where appropriate, in writing.
- Solve mathematical problems or puzzles, recognise simple patterns and relationships, generalise and predict. Suggest extensions by asking 'What if . . .?'

Differentiation

The problem on Textbook pages 7 to 10 is differentiated as follows:

More able: Problem 3 on page 9, using ThHTU.

Average: Problem 2 on page 8, using HTU.

Less able: Problem 1 on page 7, using TU.

All groups then turn to page 10 and work out a hidden message using a code.

Introducing the problem

This problem is spread over 4 pages. The first 3 pages are where the problem begins.

Explain: *The 3 knights tried to save the kingdom from the wicked dragon. Unfortunately they have ended up locked in a dungeon. Your first task is to solve some riddles that will use your knowledge of place value and number properties.*

Ask children to record the answers to the riddles on PCM 2. Explain that there is a second part to the problem, but that this can only be tackled once they have found the answers to the riddles. Children will need help here so an extra plenary or pause to explain Stage 2 (digital roots) may be advisable.

Work through this example together:
8 + 5 = 13
And 1 + 3 = 4
So the digital root of 85 is 4.

Ask:

- *Can you think of other numbers that also have a digital root of 4?*

Examples include:
13 where 1 + 3 = 4
76 where 7 + 6 = 13 and 1 + 3 = 4
22 where 2 + 2 = 4 and so on.

Teacher focus for activity

All children: Children may need some reassurance about the redundant information hidden in the riddles. Otherwise they will find that they have worked out some clues and then do not need that answer. Remind them to read each riddle all the way through and to decide what is important.

Average and More able: Children may find it helpful to have some paper for jottings as they work.

Less able: Check that children can read the riddles. If they find this difficult, read them through with the children, one riddle at a time. They should also use the digit cards and place value chart to ensure place values are correct.

Ask children questions as they work, such as:

- *How did you work that out?*
- *Is there anything in this riddle which you can ignore? How do you know that?*
- *What place does this digit have in the number?*

Optional adult input

Work with the Less able group. Check that children understand what they have to do for each riddle and use the digit cards and chart to support their place value skills.

Plenary

1   Work through some of the riddles with children, beginning with those from Textbook page 7 (Problem 1).

Ask questions such as:

- *In this riddle what can you ignore?*
- *Which clues are helpful? Are some not? Why is that?*
- *Where does this number go? How do you know that?*

2   Write the numerical answer to each riddle on the board. When all the riddles for problem 1 have been solved, with all of the children joining in, discuss how the digital root was found, and check that the children have understood this. Ask:

- *How do you find the digital root of a number?*
- *What would the digital root of 76 be?*

Children may also give 3- or 4-digit responses such as:
661 where 6 + 6 + 1 = 13 and 1 + 3 = 4
544 where 5 + 4 + 4 = 13 and 1 + 3 = 4
7942 where 7 + 9 + 4 + 2 = 22 and 2 + 2 = 4

3   Repeat this for Textbook pages 8 and 9, engaging children from all the groups in the discussion.

Ask each group for the words corresponding to their solution. How does the knight escape?

See **Useful mathematical information**, page 83 for more information on digital roots.

Development

Children could make up their own riddles where the solution is a number.

Solutions

1

Riddle	Number	Digital root
A	38	2
B	93	3
C	98	8
D	58	4

2

Riddle	Number	Digital root
A	100	1
B	111	3
C	242	8
D	123	6

3

Riddle	Number	Digital root
A	8413	7
B	5903	8
C	5864	5
D	4617	9

Clue words from Textbook
1   climb
2   look
3   up
4   chimney
5   hidden
6   ladder
7   find
8   the
9   key

The words corresponding to the digital root numbers for Problem 1 are:

2   look
3   up
8   the
4   chimney.

For Problem 2 they are: climb up the ladder (1 3 8 6).

For Problem 3 they are: find the hidden key (7 8 5 9).

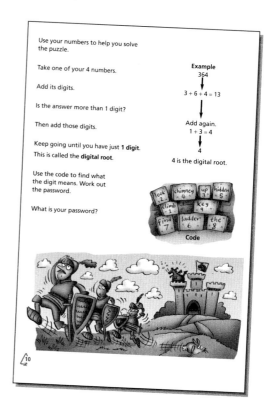

4 The skipping rope

Minimum prior experience

simple fractions; lengths in metres; addition

Resources

Textbook page 11, empty number lines (PCM 4), paper for recording, skipping ropes, string, scissors

Key vocabulary

part, fraction, whole, half, third, metre, decrease, calculate, What if . . .?

4 The skipping rope

Some children wanted to skip together, so they found a really long rope.
But half of it was rotten, so they cut off the rotten half and threw it away.
The rope was still far too long, so they cut off a third more.
They used the rest of the rope for skipping.

❶ The rope was 18 metres long to start with.
How long was their skipping rope?

❷ What if they started with 24 metres of rope?
How long would their skipping rope be?

❸ What if their skipping rope was 10 metres long?
How long was the piece of rope when they first found it?
Do you think that they could skip with a 10 metre long skipping rope?
Explain your thinking.

Draw a picture of the rope.
Draw what you know about the rope.
Think about the fractions that it is being cut into.

What's the problem?

This is a word problem that contains a lot of detail. It involves using knowledge of measures, fractions and addition to work out a given length.

Problem solving objectives

- Choose and use appropriate number operations and appropriate ways of calculating to solve problems.
- Explain methods and reasoning orally and, where appropriate, in writing.
- Solve mathematical problems or puzzles, recognise simple patterns and relationships, generalise and predict. Suggest extensions by asking 'What if . . .?'

Differentiation

The problem on Textbook page 11 is differentiated as follows:

More able: Problems 2 and 3. Children start by working out the final length, given the starting length. In problem 3 they work backwards from the final length.

Average: Problems 1 and 2. Given the starting length, children work out each finishing length.

Less able: Problem 1. Children are given a starting length of 18 m. They follow the clues to find the finishing length.

Introducing the problem

Ask children to look at the picture in their Textbook. *Have you ever tried skipping like this? Would an ordinary skipping rope be suitable? Why not?*

Discuss how a much longer rope is needed if many want to skip together. Read the problem through. *The book tells you about the skipping rope, and how long the rope is. You will need to use your knowledge of fractions in order to solve the problem.*

Ask children to decide how they will tackle the problem. Tell them that you are really interested in how they go about solving it and would like them to make a written record of what they do.

Teacher focus for activity

All children: Suggest that children draw a diagram of the rope, putting on what they know from the word problem given. They can use PCM 4 for this, or a piece of string.

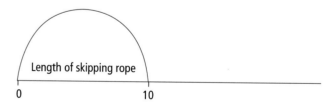

More able: Encourage children to work through the problem, but starting from the end point: how long the skipping rope is, and how that happened. It may be necessary to read the problem again.

Average and Less able: Read the problems again. Children may find it helpful to have a piece of string and scissors to model what happened to the original rope. Support children through the stages of reducing the rope by the correct fraction and amount.

As children work ask questions such as:

- *How long was the skipping rope?*
- *How was the rope cut to make the skipping rope?*

This problem really depends upon children understanding the 'story' of what happened to the rope.

Optional adult input

Work with the Less able group. Help children to model the story with a rope or a piece of string.

Plenary

1 Invite some children from each group to demonstrate the story by folding a skipping rope. Encourage them to use the language of fractions. For example: *The skipping rope was 1 full length. First, $\frac{1}{2}$ was taken away. Then, $\frac{1}{3}$ of what was left was taken away. If you calculate $\frac{2}{3}$ of the first half, you have the length of rope that remains.*

2 Explore this further. On the board, draw the original rope and write in some fractions.

3 Discuss what fraction of the whole rope is used as a skipping rope. *Half of the rope is cut into two thirds and one third. Look at the piece left over for skipping. How long is it compared to the whole piece of rope they started with?* $(\frac{1}{3})$

  See **Useful mathematical information**, page 83 on understanding fractions of quantities.

4 Invite various children to explain how they worked out their problem, and agree which ropes would be a good length for skipping and why that was. Discuss how the work was recorded and decide which methods were effective as well as efficient.

If there is a long skipping rope in school the children may enjoy the challenge of trying to skip together!

Solutions

1 The original rope was 18 m long. Half of it was cut away so that leaves 9 m. The rope was still too long, so $\frac{1}{3}$ was taken away and put in the PE store. One third of 9 m is 3 m, so that amount was taken away. The remaining $\frac{2}{3}$ will be twice as long as the part removed, so the part left over for skipping will be 6 m long.

  $18 \div 2 = 9$

  $9 - 3 = 6$

  This rope wouldn't be quite long enough for a group of 10 children. Measure the length of your arms and imagine them moving about as you jump!

2 The solution for problem 2 involves the same method as 1. The original rope is 24 m long. Removing half leaves 12 m. One third of 12 m is 4 m, so that amount was taken away. The remaining $\frac{2}{3}$ left over will be 8 m long.

  $24 \div 2 = 12$

  $12 - 4 = 8$

3 The length of skipping rope was 10 metres. This was made by cutting the rope into $\frac{1}{3}$ and $\frac{2}{3}$ pieces. The skipping rope was the longer piece. So, 10 m represents $\frac{2}{3}$ of part of the rope, the total of which would have been 15 m. The 15 metre length was made by cutting the original length of rope in two. So the original rope was 30 m long.

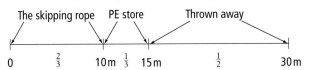

The 10 m rope should be long enough for the group of 10 children to skip together.

5 The fruit bowl

Minimum prior experience

simple fractions

Resources

Textbook page 12, paper, (bowl with plastic fruit / coloured pens / balls)

Key vocabulary

part, equal parts, fraction, one whole, half, quarter, third, calculation, total, method

5 The fruit bowl

A huge bowl is full of fresh fruit. Use the clues to work out how much fruit is in the bowl.

❶ $\frac{1}{2}$ of the fruit are apples.
There are also 2 oranges, 1 pear and 6 bananas.
How many apples are there in the bowl?
How many pieces of fruit are there altogether?

Draw a diagram, if this helps.

❷ $\frac{1}{4}$ of the fruit are apples and $\frac{1}{4}$ of the fruit are pears.
There are 6 bananas, 1 orange, 2 plums and 1 peach.
How many apples are there in the bowl?
How many pieces of fruit are there altogether?

❸ $\frac{1}{3}$ of the fruit are apples and $\frac{1}{3}$ of the fruit are pears.
There are 5 bananas, 2 oranges and 4 plums, as well as 3 strawberries and a nectarine.
How many apples are there in the bowl?
How many pieces of fruit are there altogether?
Write about how you worked out the answer.

12

What's the problem?

The bowl contains different quantities of fruit, some expressed as fractions, and some as numbers. Children are asked to work out how many pieces of particular varieties of fruit there are.

Problem solving objectives

- Choose and use appropriate number operations and appropriate ways of calculating (mental, mental with jottings, pencil and paper) to solve problems.

- Explain methods and reasoning about numbers orally and in writing.

- Solve mathematical problems or puzzles, recognise and explain patterns and relationships, generalise and predict. Suggest extensions by asking 'What if . . .?'

Differentiation

The problem on Textbook page 12 is differentiated by the fractions used:

More able: Problem 3: thirds.

Average: Problem 2: quarters.

Less able: Problem 1: halves.

Introducing the problem

Ask children to look at their Textbook page. Say that they will be expected to use their knowledge and understanding of fractions, then explain the problem to them: *You are told some information about the pieces of fruit in the fruit bowl. The problem is to work out how many apples there are, and then how many pieces of fruit there are altogether.*

Check that each ability group reads their specific problem on the page.

Explain that you are interested in how children work out their answer, and in how they record their work. Ask the children to talk through the problem with their partner, decide on how they will begin, then start the problem straight away.

Teacher focus for activity

All children: Check that children remember, for the fraction that they have for the apples, how many of these equal parts make 1 whole. Check they understand that for this problem, 1 whole refers to the total number of pieces of fruit in the bowl.

Encourage children to model the question with apparatus, if they find it difficult.

More able and Average: Children may need reminding to total the fruit where they are given quantities and relate that to a fraction.

Less able: Discuss the problem with children and ensure they understand that the fruit for which they are given quantities can be totalled. Ask: *What fraction of the whole does this represent?* (Half because the other half are apples.)

As children work, ask questions such as:

- *How many halves/quarters/thirds do you need to make one whole?*
- *How many pieces of fruit can you total? What fraction is this of all the fruit? How do you know that?*

Optional adult input

Work with the Less able group. Use the bowl and objects to demonstrate fractions of quantities, e.g. *There are 20 pens – half are red. If you know that the rest are blue, how many are each colour? (Without counting the blue pens.)*

Plenary

1 Begin with Problem 1 and invite children who worked on this problem to explain how they worked out the answer. Ask questions such as:

    How many fruits can you count in the question?

    What fraction is this of the total number of fruit? How did you work this out?

2 Draw a simple equivalence diagram for the relationships between the types of fruit.

    You may also wish to reinforce the calculation of fractions of numbers with the whole class. (See **Useful mathematical information**, page 83.)

One half	One half
Apples	2 oranges + 1 pear + 6 bananas

    Repeat this for Problems 2 and 3, asking questions such as:

    - *How can you work out how many fruit there are altogether?*
    - *What about the other fruit where you know just a fraction: how can you work out how many there are?*

3 Invite various children to show how they recorded their results and their thinking. Discuss which methods worked for them and why. Children may have:

    - drawn pictures of the fruit and totalled them;
    - written some statements about how many fruit they could count and related this to the fractions given to them.

At this stage encourage all of the More able group to write statements about what they know and show how they can find out unknowns, thinking logically. The Average ability group should be beginning to record in this way.

Solutions

1 If one half of the fruit are apples then the rest of the fruit must be one half of the total because:
$\frac{1}{2} + \frac{1}{2} = 1$
2 oranges + 1 pear + 6 bananas = 9 pieces of fruit.

You can draw a table on the board, showing what the fractions will look like.
9 is half of the total. There are 18 pieces of fruit altogether. Half are apples, so there are 9 apples.

2 If one quarter of the fruit are apples and one quarter of the fruit are pears then the rest of the fruit must be one half of the total because:
$\frac{1}{4} + \frac{1}{4} + \frac{1}{2} = 1$
6 bananas + 1 orange + 2 plums + 1 peach = 10 pieces of fruit.
10 is one half of the total. There are 20 pieces of fruit altogether. One quarter is apples, so there are 5 apples.

3 If one third of the fruit are apples and one third of the fruit are pears then the rest of the fruit must also be one third of the total because:
$\frac{1}{3} + \frac{1}{3} + \frac{1}{3} = 1$
5 bananas + 2 oranges + 4 plums + 3 strawberries + 1 nectarine = 15 pieces of fruit.
15 is one third of the total. There are 45 pieces of fruit altogether. One third is apples, so there are 15 apples.

6 Close to one hundred

6 Close to one hundred

Use these digits:

1 2 3 4 5 6

and + and =

Find totals that are **as close to 100** as possible.

You must use **all of the digits only once**. You can use the digits in **any order, each time.**

You can use digits to make 2-digit numbers, e.g. 12 + 43.

You can use them as they are, e.g. 5 + 3 + 4 + 2.

Record your calculation each time.

Here are some examples:

13 + 42 + 56 = 111

65 + 43 + 12 = 120

Which pair of digits makes the largest number? Which pair of digits makes the smallest number? Which digits can you add to give 0 for the units?

Minimum prior experience

addition of single digits and tens

Resources

Textbook page 13, Hundred squares (PCM 5), PCM 6, pencil and paper / mini whiteboards for jottings and own number lines

Key vocabulary

add, sum, total, altogether, increase, method, operation, mental, make a statement

What's the problem?

The problem involves using the digits 1, 2, 3, 4, 5 and 6 to make single and 2-digit numbers; these are added together to try to make totals as close to 100 as possible.

Problem solving objectives

- Choose and use appropriate number operations and appropriate ways of calculating (mental, mental with jottings, pencil and paper) to solve problems.

- Explain methods and reasoning orally and, where appropriate, in writing.

- Solve mathematical problems or puzzles, recognise simple patterns and relationships, generalise and predict. Suggest extensions by asking 'What if . . .?'

Differentiation

The activity on Textbook page 13 is for the whole class and is differentiated by outcome.

If children are unfamiliar with totalling numbers to 100, begin by asking them to find a total nearest to 50.

Introducing the problem

On the board write the digits 1, 2, 3, 4, 5 and 6, and the signs + and =. Explain: *This problem is about using all of these digits each time to try to make a number sentence that has a total as close to 100 as possible. You can combine any 2 digits to make a 2-digit number and must use all of the digits only once each time. Record each try on PCM 6.*

Ask children to discuss how they will go about this in their pairs, and then start the activity immediately. Allow children to use a 100 square or an empty number line to aid their calculations.

Teacher focus for activity

All children: If necessary, remind children that any 2 of these digits can be combined to make a 2-digit number. Also remind them that each digit must be used and only once.

More able: Encourage children to use mental and pencil and paper methods, and to record their number sentence, plus any workings, on PCM 6.

Average and Less able: Decide whether to suggest to children that they use a 100 square or own number lines to help them to calculate the total of 2-digit numbers. Check that children understand how to count on in 10s, then in 1s, using the 100 square.

Ask questions as children work, such as:

- *Why have you combined this pair of digits?*
- *What else have you tried?*
- *What could you try next?*
- *What do you need to add/subtract from this total to make 100? How did you work that out?*

Optional adult input

Work with the More able group. Encourage them to use and explain, mental methods to calculate, and to discuss the relationship between the numbers, why there is no point in adding certain numbers together, and what their intentions are when they combine digits.

Plenary

1 Invite some of the children to write a number sentence on the board where the answer is as close to 100 as possible. Discuss how children totalled the numbers that they chose.

2 Demonstrate the empty number line method of addition if the children need help with this, or let them show how it is used on the board, if they have found it successful. Remind them that this method involves using a combination of mental and pencil and paper calculations.

For $61 + 23 + 4 + 5$
$= 61 + 20 + 3 + 4 + 2 + 3 = 93$

3 Discuss how, with this method, it is useful to begin with the largest number, then to add 10s, then to split the units to make convenient tens such as splitting 5 into $2 + 3$ in order to reach 90, then adding on the 3. See **Useful mathematical information**, page 83, for more discussion on the use of the empty number line.

4 Discuss how the zero in the units could be obtained. One method is to total $5 + 2 + 3$. However, this will not give 100 because the other digits would have to be tens, that is $45 + 62 + 13$, for example. Discuss whether it matters which tens digit belongs to which unit:

● $15 + 42 + 63 = 120$

● $45 + 62 + 13 = 120$

● $65 + 43 + 12 = 120$

Similarly, for other ways of making zero in the units, such as $4 + 1 + 5$, the tens numbers would give, for example, $24 + 31 + 65$ which gives a total of 120.

Invite children to explain how they chose which digits to combine in order to make their number sentences.

Development

Decide whether to use some different digits, such as 1, 3, 4, 7, 8, 9, in the same way, and again to make the closest totals to 100, in class or as a homework activity. This could be simplified for the Less able group, who could have 50 as their target number. All children can use the empty number line approach when they cannot work out their total mentally.

Solutions

There are many different solutions to this. Here are some of them. The children will probably find more! It does not seem possible to make exactly 100. However, it is possible to make 102 in many different ways. For example:

$12 + 34 + 56 = 102$
$56 + 43 + 2 + 1 = 102$
$56 + 34 + 12 = 102$
$65 + 23 + 14 = 102$
$65 + 32 + 4 + 1 = 102$
$61 + 34 + 5 + 2 = 102$
$62 + 31 + 5 + 4 = 102$
$63 + 25 + 14 = 102$
$41 + 52 + 6 + 3 = 102$
$42 + 51 + 6 + 3 = 102$
$52 + 43 + 1 + 6 = 102$
$52 + 34 + 16 = 102$
$52 + 36 + 14 = 102$
$65 + 32 + 14 = 111$
$12 + 43 + 56 = 111$

Target total of 50
The nearest total is 48. It can be made in a number of ways, e.g.
$34 + 1 + 2 + 5 + 6 = 48$
$13 + 24 + 5 + 6 = 48$

7 Which way round?

7 Which way round?

You need a set of 1 to 9 digit cards.

❶ Choose any 2 digits.
  Make a number.
  Now swap over the digits to make a new number.
  Add your 2 numbers together.
  Try again for other numbers.
  What do you notice?
  Write down a rule.

  Try digits 1, 2, 3, 4 and 5 first.

❷ Choose any 3 digits.
  Make a number.
  Now reverse the digits to make a new number.
  Add your 3 numbers together to make a total.
  Try again for other numbers.
  What do you notice?
  Write down a rule.

  Set out your work in an organised way. Can you see any patterns?

14

Minimum prior experience

addition of 2-digit numbers (Less able and Average groups) and 3-digit numbers (More able group)

Resources

Textbook page 14, empty number lines (PCM 4), Hundred squares (PCM 5), Digit cards 0–9 (PCM 7)

Key vocabulary

add, addition, more, plus, sum, total, altogether, calculate, number sentence, justify

What's the problem?

Children take a number, reverse its digits to make a new number and add the 2 numbers together. They will practise adding mentally and with pencil and paper. They will notice a similarity in their results as they try different starting digits and are asked to find the pattern.

Problem solving objectives

- Choose and use appropriate number operations and appropriate ways of calculating to solve problems.
- Explain methods and reasoning orally and, where appropriate, in writing.
- Solve mathematical problems or puzzles, recognise simple patterns and relationships, generalise and predict. Suggest extensions by asking 'What if . . .?'
- Investigate a general statement about familiar numbers by finding examples that satisfy it.

Differentiation

Differentiation is by number of digits and by resources used:

More able: Problem 2: 3-digit addition using empty number lines.

Average: Problem 1: 2-digit addition using empty number lines.

Less able: Problem 1: 2-digit addition using 100 square / number lines.

Introducing the problem

On the board write the digits 2 and 3. *Which two 2-digit numbers can we make with these digits?* Write down 23 and 32 in a sum:

$$23 + 32 =$$

Invite answers from children. Explain that they will be investigating what happens when you make a number, reverse its digits and total the 2 numbers. Ask children to try different numbers and to write a rule for what they observe.

Check that each ability group knows how many digits to use each time: 3 for the More able group and 2 for the other children.

Remind children that you will be very interested in how they record their work.

Teacher focus for activity

All children: Check that children have understood what 'reverse' means. For example, for a 3-digit number such as 234, it becomes 432. Encourage the children to use mental calculation strategies where possible.

More able: Ask children to use digits which will not cross the tens or hundreds boundaries such as 1, 2, 3; 2, 3, 4 . . . They may find it helpful to use their own number line to total the numbers where their mental calculation strategies need support.

Average: Encourage children to begin with digits which will not cross the tens boundaries such as 1, 2, 3, 4 . . . They may find it helpful to use their own number line to total the numbers where their mental calculation strategies need support.

Less able: Encourage children to use 2 digits which will not cross the tens boundaries such as 1, 2, 3, 4 . . . They may need to use digit cards initially, to ensure correct placing of digits when reversed. They may also like to use a 100 square or number line to total the numbers where their mental strategies need support.

Ask questions as the children work, such as:

- *What would the number be if you reversed those digits?*
- *What have you noticed about the total?*
- *What do you think the rule is? How can you test that?*

Optional adult input

Work with the More able group. See if they begin to notice any patterns and encourage them to think about the difference between using digits which do not cross the tens or hundreds boundaries (1, 2, 3, 4) and those that do.

Plenary

1 Invite the Less able group to give some examples of the addition number sentences they tried. They can write these on the board. For example, for the digits 1 and 2:
12 + 21 = 33

Ask:

- *What do you notice about the total?*
- *Why do you think the tens and the units digits are the same?*

Children will give a rule, such as: *The digits in the tens column and in the units column are the same so the total has the same digit in both the tens and the units.*

2 Invite the Average ability group to give some examples where the totals cross the tens boundaries. For example:

Ask:

- *What do you notice about these totals?*
- *Why do you think that is?*

Children should notice that the addition, for example of 56 + 65 gives:
50 + 60 + 6 + 5 = 110 + 11 = 121

and for 87 + 78:
80 + 70 + 7 + 8 = 150 + 15 = 165

3 Discuss how the same digits appear in working out the answer, but that their place value alters their total value. For example, 50 + 60 gives 110 and 6 + 5 gives 11.

Ask children to give a rule for these addition number sentences. They may say, for example: *The total of the units gives the same digits as the total for the tens, but the place value makes the numbers have a different value.*

4 Now invite the More able group to provide some examples of 3-digit numbers, where the totals do not cross the tens or hundreds. For example:
123 + 321 = 444
Ask children to give a rule for these. Their rules will be similar to the 2-digit example above. They may also state that if you use digits which do not cross the tens boundary, then the total becomes a 'palindrome' – the same read from left to right as right to left, e.g. 143 + 341 = 484 or 543 + 345 = 888

5 Invite children to show how they recorded their results. Encourage the systematic recording of addition number sentences that children tried.

Discuss the effectiveness of the resources that children used to calculate their totals.

Ask:

- *How did you use your resource?*
- *Can you explain how you worked through a problem with it?*

Provide an example of using the empty number line with hundreds, tens and units, such as:
543 + 345.

Show another example of using the empty number line, this time with 2-digit addition, such as 25 + 52. See **Useful mathematical information**, page 83 for further advice on the use of the empty number line.

Solutions

See discussion of patterns in **Plenary**.

8 Largest and smallest totals

8 Largest and smallest totals

You need a set of 0 to 9 digit cards.

❶ Choose 4 cards.
Make two 2-digit numbers.
Make an addition sentence like this:

`3` `4` + `2` `5` =

What is the largest total that you can make with your 4 digit cards?
What is the smallest?
Try different choices of 4 cards.
Write down rules for making the largest and smallest totals.

Where should the largest digit go? And the smallest digit?

❷ Choose 6 cards.
Make two 3-digit numbers.
Make an addition sentence like this:

`3` `7` `1` + `5` `2` `8` =

What is the largest total that you can make with your 6 digit cards?
What is the smallest?
Investigate this, trying different choices of 6 cards.
Write down some rules for making the largest and smallest totals.

15

Minimum prior experience

addition of 2- and 3-digit numbers.

Resources

Textbook page 15, Digit cards 0–9 (PCM 7) for each pair, PCM 8, PCM 9, 0–100 number line (PCM 13 and 14)

Key vocabulary

add, more, plus, sum, total, altogether, increase, place value, explain your rule

What's the problem?

Children investigate the largest and smallest addition number sentences that can be made with given digits and explain how the position of certain digits influences the total.

Problem solving objectives

- Choose and use appropriate number operations and ways of calculating (mental, mental with jottings, pencil and paper) to solve problems.

- Explain methods and reasoning orally and, where appropriate, in writing.

- Solve mathematical problems or puzzles, recognise simple patterns and relationships, generalise and predict. Suggest extensions by asking 'What if . . .?'

- Investigate a general statement about familiar numbers or shapes by finding examples that satisfy it.

Differentiation

The activity on Textbook page 15 is differentiated by number of digits and by resources used:

More able: Problem 2: 3-digit addition (PCM 8) using empty number lines.

Average: Problem 1: 2-digit addition (PCM 9) using empty number lines.

Less able: Problem 1: 2-digit addition (PCM 9) using a 0–100 number line.

Introducing the problem

Explain the problem. *Shuffle the digit cards and place them in a stack face down. Choose some cards and make 2 numbers with them.* Tell children whether they choose 6 cards to make two 3-digit numbers, or 4 cards to make two 2-digit numbers. *You should add the numbers that you have made. Investigate how to place the digits that you have chosen so that you make the largest total, then the smallest.*

Ask children to write down each number sentence that they make on the PCM so that they keep a record of what they have tried. When children are clear about what to do, ask them to find a rule for making the largest total, and a rule for making the smallest total.

Provide copies of PCM 8 or PCM 9 for recording. Tell children to begin straight away.

Teacher focus for activity

All children: As children work, encourage them to use mental calculation strategies.

More able and Average: Children may find using the empty number lines helpful as an aid to calculation when they find the numbers too large for mental methods. If necessary remind them how to use an empty number line.

Less able: Children will find the 0–100 number line useful as an aid to calculation when they find the numbers too large for mental methods. If necessary remind them how to use the number line starting with adding the 10s, then the units.

As children work ask questions such as:

- *What would happen to the total if you put that digit in the hundreds/tens/units? Why?*

- *How do you think you can make the largest/smallest total?*

Optional adult input

Ask the adult to work with the Average ability group and help them to use the empty number line.

Plenary

(Have PCMs 8 and 9 set out on the board, with the digit boxes and a space for the rule.)

1   Invite the Less able and Average groups to explain what they found out. Encourage children to give examples of number sentences that they made, which can be written on to the board. Check if they can explain any rule that they have come up with.

Check whether children discovered that by placing the larger digits as tens, and smaller digits as units, they could make the greatest total.

2   Ask children to help you to work through an example.
Let's choose 4 digits. How about 1, 2, 3 and 4? How can I make the largest total? Encourage children to think about making the largest 2-digit numbers, so that the 3 and 4 become the tens numbers. Write on the board:
41 + 32 = 73

Ask:

- *Does it matter if we have 42 and 31 instead? Does that make any difference?*

Allow thinking time. Children should notice that:

- the largest 2 digits are needed to form the 2 tens digits;

- the unit digits are interchangeable as their placing makes no difference to the total.

Ask children to give the rule for making the largest possible total: the 2 larger numbers form the tens digits and the two smaller digits form the units digits.
42 + 31 = 73

3   Now invite children to suggest how to make the smallest possible total using the same digits of 1, 2, 3, 4. Children should realize here that the larger digits must be units and the smaller digits must be tens:
14 + 23 = 37
or 13 + 24 = 37

Invite children to explain why the units can 'belong' to either of the tens digits.

Ask children to provide the rule for making the smallest possible total.

4   Repeat this process with the whole class, focusing on the More able group using 3-digit numbers. Invite children to explain their rules.

Again, provide examples for all children to see. Make the examples as simple as possible, using smaller digits, so that the Less able group can follow what is happening. For example, with the digits 1, 2, 3, 4, 5, 6 and making the largest possible total:
642 + 531 = 1173
and 631 + 542 = 1173
and 641 + 532 = 1173
and 632 + 541 = 1173

5   Discuss how the largest 2 digits must form the hundreds digits; the next pair the tens, and the smallest 2 digits the units. Again, it is the place value of the digits which matters, rather than a specific calculation being formed. See **Useful mathematical information**, pages 83–84 for further discussion on making the largest and smallest possible totals.

Repeat this for producing the smallest possible total in the same way. For 1, 2, 3, 4, 5, 6:
135 + 246 = 381
and 136 + 245 = 381
and 145 + 236 = 381
and 146 + 235 = 381

Congratulate the children on their hard work.

Solutions

See **Plenary** for possible solutions.

9 Total thirty-one

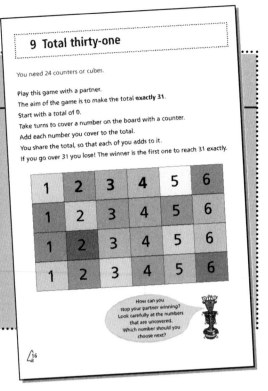

9 Total thirty-one

You need 24 counters or cubes.

Play this game with a partner.
The aim of the game is to make the total **exactly 31**.
Start with a total of 0.
Take turns to cover a number on the board with a counter.
Add each number you cover to the total.
You share the total, so that each of you adds to it.
If you go over 31 you lose! The winner is the first one to reach 31 exactly.

How can you stop your partner winning? Look carefully at the numbers that are uncovered. Which number should you choose next?

Minimum prior experience

addition of small numbers

Resources

Textbook page 16, PCM 10, counters, paper for recording

Key vocabulary

add, sum, altogether, running total, increase, more, calculate, mental calculation

What's the problem?

This is a game that involves making a running total from the mental addition of small numbers; players try to be the first to make the total 31.

Problem solving objectives

- Choose and use appropriate number operations and ways of calculating to solve problems.
- Explain methods and reasoning orally and in writing.
- Solve mathematical problems or puzzles, recognise simple patterns and relationships, generalise and predict. Suggest extensions by asking 'What if . . .?'
- Investigate a general statement about familiar numbers or shapes by finding examples that satisfy it.

Differentiation

The activity on Textbook page 16 is differentiated by outcome.

Introducing the problem

Work with your partner. Take it in turns to cover a number on the game board, and add on your number to the total. Both of you add to the same total. The first player to make the total exactly 31 wins.

Children may find it useful to use PCM 10 to record their running totals. Explain to the children that a 'running total' is where they add to a number and continually add to the new total they have created.

Remind children that you would like them to find ways of winning the game. Tell them that they will have about 15 minutes to play, and work out how they could win, then they will swap partners to test their method.

Teacher focus for activity

All children: Check that the pairs of children understand that they are both contributing to the same running total.

More able: The addition is simple, and children should do this quickly as a mental calculation. Encourage them to play the game a number of times, and try out different strategies so they can test their ideas for winning.

Average: Children should be able to calculate their running score mentally. Encourage them to think about how they might win the game, and to think of a strategy that they try out.

Less able: Children may need to write down some of their calculations, particularly when the running total is beyond 20. Encourage them to decide on a strategy and try it out. They could use an empty number line to support adding strategies.

Ask questions as children work, such as:

- *What did you try?*
- *Were you successful? Why do you think that was?*
- *What will you try next?*

Optional adult input

Work with the Less able group. Children could play as 2 larger teams against each other, and try to find a way of winning. Keep a running total of the scores, with children doing the calculation mentally, and explaining how they worked out the total. When they move from teams to pairs, they could use a number line to 31 to support their counting on and addition skills.

Plenary

1 Give children about 10 minutes of trying their strategies with a different partner.

Ask:

● *How can you be sure of winning this game?*

● *Did your idea work?*

2 Try out some of the strategies that children suggest, with the class playing the game in 2 teams, each team with a leader, preferably from different groups. A simple game board can be drawn, and numbers crossed through as they are chosen. Team leaders can take turns to keep the running total.

Ask:

● *What would happen if all the 1s and 2s were taken first? Could you win then?*

● *What if the larger numbers were taken first?*

● *Using the numbers 1, 2, 3, 4, 5 and 6, tell me some ways to make the total 31.*

Children may suggest some of the following ways of totalling 31:
6 + 6 + 6 + 6 + 5 + 2
5 + 5 + 5 + 5 + 6 + 3 + 2
4 + 4 + 4 + 4 + 6 + 6 + 3

3 Discuss ways of totalling 31 that use the fewest possible numbers. Discuss what happens if all of the larger numbers have been taken. Children may notice that if the four 6s have been used, for example, then another 7 is needed, and this could be made with 5 + 2 or 3 + 4.

4 *How did you stop your partner from winning?*

Children may have realised that they must try, when they are within a small distance of 31, to leave more than the largest number left on the board. For example, if there are 3s, 4s and 5s left, it would be sensible to have a running total that is not 26, 27 or 28.

5 *What happens if we take all of the small numbers first?*

Children may realise that they could be forced into losing, because the only numbers left will take them over 31.

Development

Children may like to play the game again, this time with a different partner, so that both children in each pair come fresh to the other player's game plan.

Alternatively, children could try this game for homework. They could search for more winning strategies. **See Useful mathematical information**, page 84 for further discussion on strategies for winning mathematical games.

Solutions

There is no winning solution to this game. It is a game of strategy. Explain that it depends upon what the partner tries, and, like playing chess, it is a good idea to try to look ahead to what might happen next.

Possible solutions include:
6 + 5 + 4 + 3 + 4 + 5 + 4
5 + 5 + 5 + 5 + 6 + 3 + 2
4 + 4 + 4 + 4 + 6 + 6 + 3
2 + 3 + 4 + 5 + 6 + 6 + 5

There are many others. Check children's suggestions as a class, or ask them to check each others. You may like to use this opportunity to discuss mental methods such as finding pairs that make 10.

10 Telephone numbers

10 Telephone numbers

Jane looked at the buttons on the telephone.
She used the buttons to work out a number for her name.
This is how she did it:

J + A + N + E
5 + 2 + 6 + 3 = 16

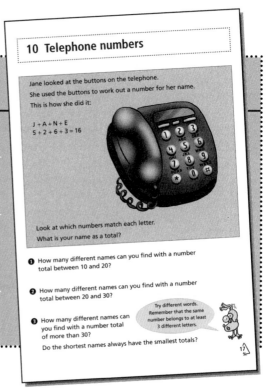

Look at which numbers match each letter.
What is your name as a total?

❶ How many different names can you find with a number total between 10 and 20?

❷ How many different names can you find with a number total between 20 and 30?

❸ How many different names can you find with a number total of more than 30?

Try different words. Remember that the same number belongs to at least 3 different letters.

Do the shortest names always have the smallest totals?

Minimum prior experience

adding several small numbers

Resources

Textbook page 17, paper for jottings/number lines, Hundred squares (PCM 5)

Key vocabulary

add, more, plus, make, sum, total, altogether, score, calculate, mental calculation, method, number sentence

What's the problem?

This activity involves addition of small numbers. These numbers are found on the telephone key pad.

Problem solving objectives

- Choose and use appropriate number operations and appropriate ways of calculating (mental, mental with jottings, pencil and paper) to solve problems.
- Explain methods and reasoning orally and, where appropriate, in writing.
- Solve mathematical problems or puzzles, recognise simple patterns and relationships, generalise and predict. Suggest extensions by asking 'What if . . .?'

Differentiation

The activity on Textbook page 17 is differentiated by the size of the number total:

More able: Problem 3: more than 30.

Average: Problem 2: 20 to 30.

Less able: Problem 1: 10 to 20.

Introducing the problem

Ask children to look at the page in their Textbooks and then explain the problem.

Jane looked at the buttons on the telephone. She used the buttons to work out a number for her name. This is how she did it.

Write on the board:
J + A + N + E
5 + 2 + 6 + 3 = 16

Children may find it helpful to begin by finding the number total for their own first names, so that they understand how this works.

Explain to children that they should find as many names as they can within their number range.

Ask children to decide, with their partner, how they will solve the problem. Explain that you will be interested in how they record their results. Ask them to start straight away.

Teacher focus for activity

All children: Check that children understand that a number on the telephone pad, apart from 0 and 1, has 3 or 4 letters associated with it. In order to find as many names' totals as possible, children will need to have good rapid recall of the totals of small numbers.

More able: Encourage children to think about how they can find larger totals. They may suggest using longer names, finding names with more letters from towards the end of the alphabet, or using both strategies. Encourage children to record all of the names that they try.

Average: Children may find it helpful to begin with the names of their family and friends. Discuss with them what is likely to happen if they choose names with 4, 5, 6 . . . letters.

Less able: Encourage children to begin with names that have 3 or 4 letters, such as Ben, Jan, Jack . . .

Optional adult input

Work with the Less able group. First, work altogether, recording the names that they suggest and the name number. Then help children to work individually, using a number line or 100 square, if necessary.

Plenary

1 Ask each group in turn to provide some names, their calculation and the total. Children can write these on the board for others to see. As children provide answers, there will be names that have the same total, such as Naima and David (see **Solutions**, below).

   Say:

   ● *These names are very different. Why do they have the same total?*

   Children may notice some similarities in the numbers. Re-write the numbers, in number order. For example, for David and Naima:
   David $2 + 3 + 3 + 4 + 8$
   Naima $2 + 2 + 4 + 6 + 6$

2 Ask children to comment on what they notice. They may say:

   ● Both names have 2 sets of numbers that total 10 ($3 + 3 + 4$; $8 + 2$ for David; $4 + 6$; $2 + 2 + 6$ for Naima).

   ● Even though the digits are not the same, they have the same differences in value, so create an identical total.

3 Encourage children to spot number properties. For example, they may notice in a name such as Jill that there are 3 odd numbers, and 1 even number. Encourage the children to make generalisations about the numbers, such as: where there is an odd number of odd numbers and even numbers, the total will be odd.

   Also, ask children from the More able group to explain methods such as longer names or names with more letters towards the end of the alphabet. What did they find?

   Children may want to add more names, and their totals. Ask:

   ● *What is the largest/smallest name total that you have found?*

   ● *Is it always longer names which give a higher total? Why/Why not?*

4 Discuss how children went about the task and how they recorded what they found out. Some children may have recorded their results in a table. Some may have tried to record them so that the names were in number total order.

See **Useful mathematical information**, page 84 for further information on telephone key pads and letters and corresponding numbers.

Development

Ask children to try to find the name with the smallest/biggest possible total:

Can anyone find a name which has a single-digit total? Can anyone find a name with a total of more than 35?

Or children could find out whose name in the class gives the highest/lowest total. They can do these activities individually, or the More able group can support the Less able group.

For homework, children could use family and friends' surnames, and find the name with the smallest and largest totals.

Solutions

Here are some names with their totals:

Name	Sum	Total
Ben	$2 + 3 + 6$	11
Yi	$9 + 4$	13
Jack	$5 + 2 + 2 + 5$	14
May	$6 + 2 + 9$	17
Wen	$9 + 3 + 6$	18
Deepa	$3 + 3 + 3 + 7 + 2$	18
Jill	$5 + 4 + 5 + 5$	19
Naima	$6 + 2 + 4 + 6 + 2$	20
David	$3 + 2 + 8 + 4 + 3$	20
John	$5 + 6 + 4 + 6$	21
Megan	$6 + 3 + 4 + 2 + 6$	21
Sarah	$7 + 2 + 7 + 2 + 4$	22
Jody	$5 + 6 + 3 + 9$	23
Emily	$3 + 6 + 4 + 5 + 9$	27
Zeeman	$9 + 3 + 3 + 6 + 2 + 6$	29
Milly	$6 + 4 + 5 + 5 + 9$	29
Joshua	$5 + 6 + 7 + 4 + 8 + 2$	32
Thomas	$8 + 4 + 6 + 6 + 2 + 7$	33
Preyasi	$7 + 7 + 3 + 9 + 2 + 7 + 4$	39
Stephen	$7 + 8 + 3 + 7 + 4 + 3 + 6$	38
Elizabeth	$3 + 5 + 4 + 9 + 2 + 2 + 3 + 8 + 4$	40
Christopher	$2 + 4 + 7 + 4 + 7 + 8 + 6 + 7 + 4 + 3 + 7$	59

11 Make a number

Minimum prior experience

addition and subtraction of 2-digit numbers

Resources

Textbook page 18, Hundred squares (PCM 5), 0–100 number lines (PCM 13 and 14)

Key vocabulary

add, addition, sum, total, altogether, increase, subtract, take away, minus, difference, method

11 Make a number

Find different ways of making your total.
You can use addition and subtraction (+ or –).
You can use the same number only **once** in any calculation.

❶ These are your numbers: 1 3 5 15 17 19 36
Find different ways of totalling **40**.

❷ These are your numbers: 5 17 19 37 39 46 66
Find different ways of totalling **100**.

❸ These are your numbers: 10 17 27 45 48 83 85
Find different ways of totalling **120**.

Which way uses the fewest of these numbers to make your total?
Which way uses the most of these numbers to make your total?

Choose pairs of numbers.
What totals can you make?
What is the difference between them?
Now try choosing 3 numbers.

18

What's the problem?

Children try to reach different totals, by adding or subtracting given 1- and 2-digit numbers.

Problem solving objectives

- Choose and use appropriate number operations and appropriate ways of calculating (mental, mental with jottings, pencil and paper) to solve problems.
- Explain methods and reasoning orally and, where appropriate, in writing.
- Solve mathematical problems or puzzles, recognise simple patterns and relationships, generalise and predict. Suggest extensions by asking 'What if . . .?'

Differentiation

The problem on Textbook page 18 is differentiated by outcome and resources used:

More able: Problem 3: Make 120; pencil and paper.

Average: Problem 2: Make 100; pencil and paper and 100 square, 0–100 number line.

Less able: Problem 1: Make 40; pencil and paper, 100 square, 0–100 number line.

Introducing the problem

Explain the problem: *You will have a target number of 40, 100 or 120. You are given a list of numbers that you have to use to reach your target number. You can use any of the numbers in a calculation, but only once. You can add and subtract, and use combinations of adding and subtracting.*

Ask children to discuss the problem with their partner and to decide how they will go about solving it. Explain that you are expecting children to think about what they do before they start the problem, and that they should write down which methods and equipment they will use to help them add and subtract.

Ask them to begin the problem immediately.

Teacher focus for activity

All children: Check that children have decided how to tackle the problem and that they have decided which resources and methods will help them with adding and subtracting.

More able: Encourage children to use mental and paper and pencil methods, and to show their working on paper.

Average and Less able: Children may find the 100 square a useful resource for helping them to calculate addition and subtraction. Remind them how to count in 10s and 1s to add and subtract using the 100 square. Alternatively, a 0–100 number line could be used.

As children work, ask questions such as:

- *Which combinations have you tried?*
- *What could you try next?*
- *What do you need to add to/take away from this total to make 100? How did you work that out?*

Optional adult input

Work with the Less able group. Working together, use an A3 enlargement of the 100 square for counting on and back to calculate additions and subtractions. Support them with questions as above. You could also introduce and explain the number line method, or encourage its use if children are already familiar with it. They could use the number line in pairs or individually.

Plenary

1   Allow children to read out their intended method that they wrote initially. Discuss how methods might change as they carry out the investigation, and that there is nothing wrong with this.

2   Invite children to share their responses. They can write their solutions on the board. Ask:

   ● *How did you work this out?*

   Encourage children to explain their thinking.

   The Average group may have noticed for example:

   ● $37 + 17 = 54$. They should recognise that to make 100 the unit number must be 6, so that $54 + 46 = 100$

   ● $66 + 39$ results in a 5 in the units so $66 + 39 = 105$, but there is a 5 available, so they could finish with $105 - 5 = 100$

   Allow children from each group to feed back their answers. Discuss methods used.

3   Encourage the Less able group to explain the number line method, if they have used it.

   Check that children understand how to use an empty number line as a means of calculating addition and subtraction with 2-digit numbers.

   For $39 + 17 = 39 + 10 + 1 + 6 = 56$

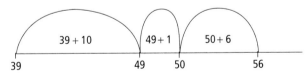

   and

   For $66 - 37 = 66 - 30 - 6 - 1 = 29$

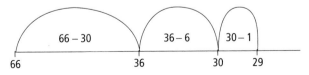

Use the empty number line approach for more examples of working out addition and subtraction of 2-digit numbers, as this is a mental with pencil and paper strategy that children will find very useful. See also **Useful mathematical information**, page 83 for further discussion on using empty number lines.

4   Discuss how children recorded their number sentences. Discuss different methods used. For example, some children may have grouped them, showing where there were 3 numbers used, and so on. Ask children if they recorded number sentences that did not total their target number. Suggest to them that it is useful to record all working, so that they have a written record of what they have tried and can then work out what they still need to try.

Solutions

Here are 2 possible ways of creating each total. The children will probably find more!

1   **40:**
   $17 + 19 + 3 + 1 = 40$
   $15 + 5 + 19 + 1 = 40$

2   **100:**
   $46 + 37 + 17 = 100$
   $66 + 19 + 37 - 17 - 5 = 100$

3   **120:**
   $45 + 85 - 10 = 120$
   $45 + 48 + 27 = 120$

12 Shoes, dogs and cats

Minimum prior experience

addition and subtraction of small numbers

Resources

Textbook pages 19 and 20, paper

Key vocabulary

add, sum, total, altogether, subtract, take away, leave, difference, double counting, jotting, answer, justify, make a statement

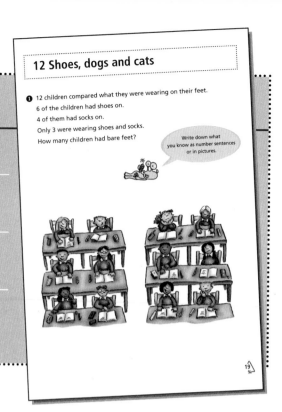

12 Shoes, dogs and cats

❶ 12 children compared what they were wearing on their feet.
6 of the children had shoes on.
4 of them had socks on.
Only 3 were wearing shoes and socks.
How many children had bare feet?

Write down what you know as number sentences or in pictures.

19

What's the problem?

Information is given about the number of people, dogs or cats who wear or like particular things. Using logic, children work out how many belong to each group.

Problem solving objectives

- Choose and use appropriate number operations and ways of calculating to solve problems.
- Explain methods and reasoning orally and, where appropriate, in writing.
- Solve mathematical problems or puzzles, recognise simple patterns and relationships, generalise and predict. Suggest extensions by asking 'What if . . .?'

Differentiation

The activities on Textbook pages 19 and 20 are for the whole class, and are differentiated by outcome.

Introducing the problem

Read Problem 1 through with the class. Inform children that Problems 2 and 3 are similar, even though they are about cats and dogs.

Ask children to begin by discussing the problem with their partner and decide how they will proceed. Explain that you are as interested in how they go about the problem as in the answer, and ask them to keep a careful record of what they decide to do.

Teacher focus for activity

All children: Each problem depends upon logical thinking. The numbers involved are very small, so the arithmetic is easy for everyone. Encourage children to talk through and record, in some way, what they already know about each problem.

More able: Suggest that children write some number sentences to show what they know. They can also write some sentences using a symbol such as a square to represent what they do not know yet. A simple Venn Diagram could be encouraged (See **Optional adult input**).

Average and Less able: Suggest that children record what they already know, either by writing number sentences or by drawing pictures to represent the data. Ask them to identify what they do not know yet and decide how they could find this out. They might try using small numbers until they find a number that fits, for example.

Ask questions as children work, such as:
- *What do you already know?*
- *What do you have to find out?*
- *How could you do that?*

Optional adult input

Work with the More able group. Encourage them to write number sentences and begin to use symbols and numbers, to represent the information. A simple Venn Diagram could be drawn, showing the

44

❷ There are 11 dogs.
4 dogs love 'Doggy bites' dog biscuits.
3 dogs enjoy 'Woof 'em down' dog biscuits.
Only 2 of these dogs will eat both 'Doggy bites' and 'Woof 'em down' dog biscuits.
The other dogs will only eat 'Growly' dog biscuits.
How many dogs will only eat 'Growly' dog biscuits?

❸ Mrs Jordan has 15 cats. They like different flavours of cat food.
Some of them will only eat fish.
8 of them like rabbit.
4 of the cats prefer chicken.
1 cat eats both rabbit and chicken.
How many cats will only eat fish?

intersecting group with socks and shoes, and used to help calculate the answer.

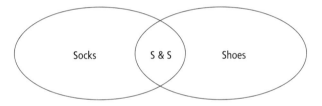

Plenary

1 Focus on Problem 1. Ask children about the story in the Textbook. Say:

- *Did you use everything that the story told you?*

- *What was not important to the problem? Why was that?*

2 Invite children from each group to explain how they went about solving the problem. They may have:

- drawn pictures about children to show what they are wearing;

- tried different numbers in number sentences to try to find numbers that fit what they know.

3 Discuss strategies that children tried, and encourage discussion about what worked well or not. Talk about how, in problems like this one, it can be necessary to try different strategies, and that some strategies may not work for a particular problem.

4 Work through some of the correct solutions that children have, and discuss how they worked out the answer to the problem. Try Problems 2 and 3.

Explain the problems to those who have not attempted them, and ask children to pair up with someone who has, so they can see methods for discussion

5 Finally, ask children what they have learnt about solving logic problems. Suggestions could include:

- *find the data that you need in a problem, and ignore what is not part of the problem;*

- *think logically;*

- *keep a record of what you do, so that if the strategy does not work, you can go back to an earlier stage and try a different way to solve the problem.*

Development

There is another example of this type of problem on page 84 of **Useful mathematical information**, which could be used to develop children's logical thinking skills. This could be used as part of a lesson or set as homework.

Solutions

Use symbols above the numerals or a Venn Diagram to illustrate how the problem can be tackled. Children will see how pictures or a diagram can aid logical thinking.

1 There are 12 children.
6 are wearing shoes and 4 are wearing socks.
3 of these 10 are wearing both.
This means there are 3 who only wear shoes and 1 who only has socks.
$3 + 3 + 1 = 7$
$12 - 7 = 5$
This means that 5 children are left, who must have bare feet.

2 There are 11 dogs.
4 love 'Doggy bites' and 3 like 'Woof em down' biscuits.
2 of this 7 like both. That means there are 2 who only eat 'Doggy' and 1 who only eats 'Woof'.
$2 + 2 + 1 = 5$
$11 - 5 = 6$
There are 6 dogs left over, so there are 6 who only eat Growly dog biscuits.

3 There are 15 cats.
8 like rabbit, 4 prefer chicken.
1 of this 12 eats both. This means there are 7 who only like rabbit and 3 who only like chicken.
$7 + 3 + 1 = 11$
$15 - 11 = 4$
There are 4 cats left over, so there are 4 who only eat fish.

13 Count down to zero

Minimum prior experience

subtraction of small numbers

Resources

Textbook page 21, PCM 12, PCM 4, transparent counters of different colours

Key vocabulary

subtract, take away, minus, difference, leave, running total, mental calculation, justify, method

13 Count down to zero

Play this game with a partner.

You need 10 counters each. Choose a different colour each.

31	30	29	28	27	26	25	24
16	17	18	19	20	21	22	23
15	14	13	12	11	10	9	8
0	1	2	3	4	5	6	7

Decide who will go first.

Player 1

Start with the number 31.

Choose a number from 1 to 4.

1 2 3 4

Take away that number from 31.

Leave a counter on the number you reach.

Player 2

Start from the counter number.

Choose a number from 1 to 4.

1 2 3 4

Count back that number.

Leave a counter on the number you reach.

Repeat, taking turns. The winner is the first person to finish on 0.

Can you find a winning strategy?

21

What's the problem?

Using the numbers 1 to 4, children work out a strategy for subtracting from 31, keeping a running total, and aiming to be the first to reach zero. They are asked to work out a strategy for winning the game. The winning strategy involves counting down in multiples of 5.

Problem solving objectives

● Choose and use appropriate number operations and ways of calculating to solve problems.

● Explain methods and reasoning orally and, where appropriate, in writing.

● Solve mathematical problems or puzzles, recognise simple patterns and relationships, generalise and predict. Suggest extensions by asking 'What if . . .?'

● Investigate a general statement about familiar numbers or shapes by finding examples that satisfy it.

Differentiation

The activity on Textbook page 21 is differentiated by outcome.

Introducing the problem

Ask children to work in pairs and play the game. Show them PCM 12 and suggest that they use this as a record sheet for their calculations. Remind them to start from 31 initially.

Find a strategy so that you can win the game. When you think you have a strategy, swap partners and play the game with someone else. Will your strategy work?

Explain that you would then like everyone to choose a different start number and check whether their strategy still works.

Ask children to start playing the game.

Teacher focus for activity

All children: As children work, ask them about their strategies. Encourage them to work cooperatively, trying out 1 strategy. They can take turns at going first. They can use a calculator for checking their partner's calculations if they wish.

More able: Encourage children to work mentally because the subtraction involved should be very simple for them. This should speed up the game, so that they can quickly record their subtractions and move to the next go.

Average: Children should be able to work mentally for each calculation. If, however, they need help, remind them of the strategies that they know.

Less able: Children can use the grid on Textbook page 21 to count back each time.

Ask questions as the children work, such as:

● *What strategy have you tried? Did it work? Why do you think it works?*

● *Does it matter who goes first?*

● *What else could you try?*

When 5 minutes remain, whisper the strategy to some children who haven't come up with one yet (i.e. what numbers to land on), and see if they can discover why it works before the plenary.

Optional adult input

Work with the Average group, and remind them of other strategies, e.g. partitioning. Help them with the subtraction calculations using the grid on Textbook page 21.

Plenary

1 Ask for suggestions for a strategy. Children may have realised that there is a key number: whoever lands on this number wins, because their partner can then only subtract insufficient for winning, leaving them enough to subtract next time.

2 Children may have tried to find a foolproof way of landing on 5, so that they would win. Ask if anyone found a way of guaranteeing that they could do this. Note that unless the child starts first this probably will not work. Play the game together, with you starting, and subtracting 1. The following are the numbers that you must land on at some time in order to win:

30   25   20   15   10   5   0

Ask:

- *What strategy did I use?*

3 Invite children to play the game again, agree who goes first, and check that this strategy wins. Ask children to explain how this strategy works. They may say:

- *Whoever goes first always lands on a number that is in the 5 times table.*

4 Explain that the numbers, if counted from zero, increase by 5 each time. The other player can only subtract 4 at most, and can't reach the important multiple of 5.

5 Ask children to try this strategy for another starting number, such as 24. Ask:

- *What would be the first important number to land on?* (20)

- *Will it matter who goes first?*

Suggest that they play this now, with their partner, and agree who will go first.

6 Try this again, for different starting numbers, so that children recognise that the important strategy is to be the first to land on a multiple of 5.

Development

As an extension to this activity, or for homework, children can play the game again, but with different small numbers to subtract. The following are suggested:

More able: 1 to 8.

Average: 1 to 5.

Less able: 1 to 4.

Strategies will again involve ensuring that the other player cannot finish the game:

More able: counting in 9s, with a sequence of:
43   36   27   18   9   0

Average: counting in 6s, with a sequence of:
43   42   36   30   24   18   12   6   0

Less able: counting in 5s, with a sequence of:
43   40   35   30   25   20   15   10   5   0

Some children, particularly the More able group, should be able to begin to make a generalised statement about this game, such as: 'Whatever run of numbers you use to subtract each time, look at one more than the greatest number, and find the counting pattern for that number, starting from zero. This will give the sequence needed to win the game'.

Solutions

See **Plenary**. Winning depends on a player realising the importance of landing on the number 5, and multiples of 5.

See **Useful mathematical information**, pages 84–85 for further discussion on winning strategies for games like this one.

14 Four in a row

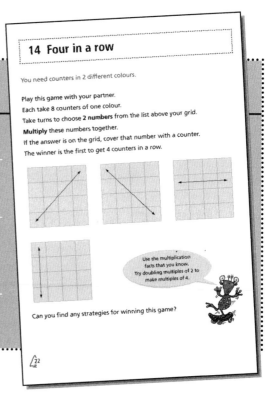

Minimum prior experience

multiplication by 2, 3, 4, 5 and 10

Resources

Textbook pages 22 and 23, 0–100 number lines (PCM 13 and 14), counters

Key vocabulary

lots of, groups of, times, product, multiply, multiplied by, multiple, mental calculation, calculate, justify

What's the problem?

The problem involves finding multiples of pairs of numbers.

Problem solving objectives

- Choose and use appropriate number operations and ways of calculating to solve problems.
- Explain methods of calculation and reasoning about numbers orally, and where appropriate, in writing.
- Solve mathematical problems or puzzles, recognise simple patterns or relationships, generalise and predict. Suggest extensions by asking 'What if . . .?'

Differentiation

The activity is differentiated by multiplications including:

More able: Problem 3: multiples of 2, 3, 4, 10, 20, 50, 95.

Average: Problem 2: multiples of 2, 3, 4, 5, 10, 15, 30.

Less able: Problem 1: multiples of 2, 3, 4, 5, 6, 7, 10.

Introducing the problem

Ask children to look at the game grids on Textbook pages 22 and 23. Explain: *You will each need 8 counters. Take turns to choose 2 numbers from the list above the grid and multiply these 2 numbers. If the answer to the calculation is on the grid, cover that number with a counter. The idea of the game is to get 4 counters in a row.*

Make it clear that you are interested in how children work out the answers, and how they tackle the problem. Encourage children to think about winning strategies.

Teacher focus for activity

All children: The game involves some multiples that children should be able to recall or calculate mentally, and others where they may need to use pencil and paper. Encourage children to use mental strategies and rapid recall where they can. They may also need to be reminded of the commutative nature of multiplication, for example that: 3×7 is the same as 7×3.

More able: Some of the multiples are outside the normal range for Year 3, in order to encourage the children to use pencil and paper strategies, as well as mental ones. Children will find it useful to keep a note of how they worked these out.

Average: Where the multiples cannot be resolved by rapid recall, such as 15×30, suggest that children break this down into smaller steps, such as 15×3 and 45×10.

Less able: Children may find it helpful to use PCM 13 and 14 to mark in the counting patterns of the multiples up to 100.

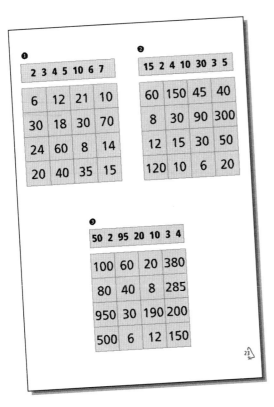

Optional adult input

Work with the Average group. Encourage children to find mental and pencil and paper methods for working out multiples that cannot be answered by rapid recall.

Plenary

1   Invite various children to explain how they played the game. Allow them to discuss the strategies that they used, such as:

- blocking their partner's next move by covering that square;

- covering squares that do not make a line in order to give different possibilities for future moves;

- looking at the multiples and working out which pairs make that number while it's not your turn;

- thinking ahead, and trying to block future moves, as well as giving more opportunities for their partner to have different moves in the future.

2   Many children will have played the counter game, or the computer version of it, and will have some ideas about winning strategies. Discuss these as a class.

3   On the board, draw one of the game grids from the Textbook and invite children to play the game. Divide the class into 2 groups, to play against each other. Invite a child from each group to choose a response from the others, and to mark the chosen solution on to the board each time. When either 1

group has won, or they have reached stalemate, invite children to explain their thinking, as they played the game.

Ask:

- *Why did you choose this square?*

- *How could you stop the other side from winning?*

- *Did you find any multiples that were not on the grid? What did you do about those numbers?*

- *Which multiples were more difficult to calculate? How did you work those out?*

When children have discussed their strategies, play another game, with the class in 2 groups as before, choosing another grid from the Textbook. Encourage children to think about possible strategies that they could use in order to win. See also **Useful mathematical information**, page 00 for strategies that could be used for multiplying larger numbers.

Solutions

Here are some possible multiples for the pairing of numbers. There are others.

Highlighted numbers are not in the grid.

1 Multiple (possible calculation)	2 Multiple (possible calculation)	3 Multiple (possible calculation)
6 (3×2)	30 (15×2)	100 (50×2)
8 (4×2)	60 (15×4)	4750 (50×95)
10 (5×2)	150 (15×10)	1000 (50×20)
20 (10×2)	450 (30×15)	500 (50×10)
12 (6×2)	45 (15×3)	150 (50×3)
14 (7×2)	75 (15×5)	200 (50×4)
12 (4×3)	8 (4×2)	190 (95×2)
15 (5×3)	20 (2×10)	40 (20×2)
30 (10×3)	60 (2×30)	20 (10×2)
18 (6×3)	6 (2×3)	6 (2×3)
21 (7×3)	10 (5×2)	8 (2×4)
20 (5×4)	40 (4×10)	1900 (95×20)
40 (10×4)	120 (30×4)	950 (95×10)
24 (6×4)	12 (4×3)	285 (95×3)
28 (7×4)	20 (4×5)	380 (95×4)
50 (10×5)	300 (10×30)	200 (20×10)
30 (6×5)	30 (10×3)	60 (20×3)
35 (7×5)	50 (10×5)	80 (20×4)
60 (10×6)	90 (30×3)	30 (10×3)
70 (10×7)	150 (30×5)	40 (10×4)
42 (7×6)	15 (3×5)	12 (4×3)

15 A pocketful of money

15 A pocketful of money

Daniel, Chloe and Harry have a lot of change in their pockets. They find a vending machine.

❶ Daniel buys a ▭. He uses up to 5 coins.
Which coins does he use?
Find different answers.

❷ Chloe buys a ▭. She uses up to 5 coins.
Which coins does she use?
Find different answers.

❸ Harry buys a ▭. He uses up to 10 coins.
Which coins does he use?
Find different answers.

24

Minimum prior experience

recognize all coins; total coins to £1

Resources

Textbook page 24, PCM 11, selection of 1p, 2p, 5p, 10p, 50p coins and £1 coins for introduction

Key vocabulary

money, coin, total, amount, value, how much . . .? how many . . .?

What's the problem?

This activity involves searching for totals of a given number of coins. Children will learn to work systematically, and will calculate different totals with varying numbers of coins (see **Differentiation**).

Problem solving objectives

- Choose and use appropriate operations to solve word problems.

- Explain methods and reasoning orally and, where appropriate, in writing.

- Solve mathematical problems or puzzles, recognise simple patterns and relationships, generalise and predict. Suggest extensions by asking 'What if . . .?'

- Solve word problems involving numbers in 'real life', money and measures, using one or more steps, including finding totals and giving change, and working out which coins to pay.

Differentiation

The lesson is differentiated by the total paid and number of coins used.

More able: Problem 3: up to 10 coins; making £1.

Average: Problem 2: up to 5 coins; making £1.

Less able: Problem 1: up to 5 coins; making 50p.

Introducing the problem

Discuss situations where change is needed, e.g. making telephone calls or buying items from a vending machine. Explain that you have some coins in your pocket. Put five coins out (1p, 2p, 10p, 20p, £1 coins) and total the coins by encouraging a child to

start with the largest value coin and then count on: *£1 and 20p is £1.20; add 10p is £1.30, add 2p is £1.32 add 1p is £1.33. If someone asked me for change for a 50p coin could I give the change? Why not?* Encourage children to explain that, although there is far more than 50p in coins, it is not possible to make **exactly** 50p with any combination of coins.

Ask children to look at the textbook page. Discuss which coins can be used and remind each group what they have to calculate. Explain to all groups that they can use as few of their coins as they wish in order to make a total, e.g. it is possible to make 50p with just 3 coins: 20p + 20p + 10p. Encourage children to think of their own way of recording. Alternatively, PCM 11 can be used to record combinations of coins.

Teacher focus for activity

All children: As children work ask questions such as:

- *Which combinations of coins have you tried?*

- *How did this help you to find a solution?*

- *What could you try next?*

More able: Ask children to suggest ways in which they can make the total of £1 from a combination of up to 10 coins. Encourage children to find as many combinations as possible and to work systematically, by, for example, changing one coin only each time.

Average: Begin by asking children to find combinations that make £1, but to record all the combinations that they try. Remind children that they do not need to use all five coins each time to make the total. Encourage children to work systematically by changing just one coin at a time.

Less able: Check that children can total the coins quickly and efficiently by working from largest to smallest, and totalling by counting on. Children should discover quite quickly that the 1p and 2p coins are not helpful because three coins are needed to make just 5p (1p + 2p + 2p) and it is then not possible to make a total of 50p.

Optional adult input

Work with the Average group. Children can begin as a group, working with the same coin combinations, then, search in pairs, for different ways of making this total with different coins.

Plenary

1 Invite children who worked on problem 1 to give some suggestions for making totals of 50p. Using an enlarged version of PCM 11, ask children to record the coins that they chose. Invite one or two of the children to demonstrate using real coins.

2 Now ask those who attempted problem 2 to explain how they tackled this. Discuss the strategies that they tried.

Ask questions such as:

● *Which coin did you start with in your counting?*

● *How did you avoid repeating a possible solution?*

● *What is the largest / smallest number of coins that you used?*

3 Now ask the group who tackled problem 3 to explain how they found solutions. Again, encourage children to demonstrate some ways of making £1. Children from other groups may wish to suggest possible ways. Children may comment on how useful a 50p coin is in finding different ways of making £1.

4 Discuss the importance of being systematic in working. Children may well have noticed how just changing one or two coins each time helps them to keep track of what they have tried, and is a pointer to what could be tried next.

See **Useful mathematical information** page 85 for more information about working systematically.

Development

For homework children could find ways of making a total of £2 using up to 8 coins.

Solutions

Here are some possible solutions to each problem:

1 Making **50p** (5 coins or fewer)
50p
20p + 20p + 10p
20p + 20p + 5p + 5p
20p + 10p + 10p + 5p + 5p

2 Making **£1** (5 coins or fewer)
50p + 50p
50p + 20p + 20p + 10p
20p + 20p + 20p + 20p + 20p
50p + 20p + 20p + 5p + 5p
50p + 20p + 10p + 10p + 10p

3 Making **£1** (10 coins or fewer)
50p + 20p + 20p + 5p + 2p + 2p + 1p
50p + 20p + 20p + 2p + 2p + 2p + 2p + 2p
50p + 20p + 10p + 10p + 5p + 2p + 1p + 1p + 1p
20p + 20p + 20p + 20p + 10p + 5p + 2p + 1p + 1p + 1p

16 Mystery numbers

Minimum prior experience

multiplication and division by 2 and 5; counting patterns in 3s and 4s; remainders

Resources

Textbook page 25, Hundred square (PCM 5), 0–50 number line (PCM 13), paper for recording, coloured pencils, large class 100 square

Key vocabulary

lots of, groups of, times, multiply, multiple, repeated addition, divide, divisible by, remainder, left over, jotting

What's the problem?

Children are asked to find numbers that can be divided exactly by 3, but when divided by 2, 4 or 5 there is a remainder of 1.

Problem solving objectives

- Choose and use appropriate number operations and appropriate ways of calculating to solve problems.
- Explain methods and reasoning about numbers orally and, where appropriate, in writing.
- Solve mathematical problems or puzzles, recognise simple patterns and relationships, generalise and predict. Suggest extensions by asking 'What if . . .?'

Differentiation

The problem is differentiated by size of number and resources used:

More able: Problems 1 and 2.

Average and Less able: Problem 1.

Introducing the problem

Ask children to suggest numbers that can be divided by 2. Write these on the board. Now ask for numbers that can be divided by 5, then 3, then 4. Now ask for a number which, when divided by 2, has a remainder of 1. (e.g. 5)

Ask class to see if they know what a remainder is.

A remainder happens when a number will not divide exactly and there is something left over. For example: 5 ÷ 2 = 2 r 1. There is 1 left over.

This puzzle is about dividing a number. When it is divided by 3 there is no remainder. When it is divided by 2, 4 or 5 there is a remainder of 1. What could that number be?

Explain to children that in Problem 1 they are searching for 1 number, and that it is less than 30. In problem 2 they need to find a different number to fit the clue. It will be more than 50 and less than 100.

Tell children that you are really interested in how they solve this puzzle. Ask them to write a sentence to explain how they calculated the solution, after they have completed it.

Teacher focus for activity

All children: Encourage children to use the multiplication and division facts that they know, and to derive those that they do not know. They may find repeated addition or subtraction from known facts helpful. (See **Useful mathematical information**, page 85).

More able: Children may find it helpful to note multiplication patterns on the 100 square, perhaps by marking the squares in a given colour according to multiplication table.

Average: Children may find it helpful to mark the multiplication tables on to a number line, using a different coloured pencil for each table. PCM 13 (0–50 line) could be used.

Less able: Children will need guidance on how to use a number line for multiplication and division. Allow them to mark on each multiplication table in a different colour, so they can identify the different multiples, beginning from zero. PCM 13 could be used.

See **Useful mathematical information**, page 85 for further information on repeated addition and using a number line as a means of devising multiplication tables and finding remainders.

As children work, ask questions such as:

- *Which numbers are in both the 2/3/4/5 and the 2/3/4/5 tables? How will that help you?*
- *Which are the numbers that give a remainder of 1 when divided by 2/4/5?*

Optional adult input

Work with the Less able group. Help them to mark all the multiplication facts up to 30. Encourage them to mark the tables in different colours, showing repeated addition as a way of calculating multiplication. Ensure they understand the concept of 'remainder', using cubes to demonstrate, if necessary, and then moving on to the number line.

Plenary

1   Draw a number line to 30. Invite the Less able group to feed back to the others how they went about solving their problem. Let children mark out how they showed different table facts on the line. Say:

- *Which numbers can be divided exactly by 2, 4 and 5?*

Children should respond with 20 and 40.

- *Which number, near to 20 but not near to 40, can be divided by 3? (21)*

2   Repeat this for the next number after 50. Let the More able group demonstrate how they found the second number. They should have found that 81 is the next number that fits the criteria.

3   Demonstrate how these 2 numbers were found using the 100 square (see **Solutions**). Invite a child to show the pattern of 2s, then 4s, then 5s, and how 20 is the first number to fit this criteria. Now invite another child to show the pattern of 3s and that 21 is the first one that will fit the criteria, because dividing 21 by 2, 4 or 5 leaves a remainder of 1.

4   On the board write:
$21 \div 2 = 10\ r\ 1$
$21 \div 3 = 7$
$21 \div 4 = 5\ r\ 1$
$21 \div 5 = 4\ r\ 1$

Explain what the 'r' means ('remainder' or left over) and show this on the number line and 100 square, so children can see how these numbers do not divide exactly and what remains.

Repeat this for the second solution number, 81.

5   Talk about how children recorded their work. Invite children to suggest different sentences explaining why their solution fitted the criteria.

Solutions

The solutions are 21 and 81.

Look at the table.

1	2	3	4	5	6	7	8	9	10
11	12	13	14	15	16	17	18	19	20
21	22	23	24	25	26	27	28	29	30
31	32	33	34	35	36	37	38	39	40
41	42	43	44	45	46	47	48	49	50
51	52	53	54	55	56	57	58	59	60
61	62	63	64	65	66	67	68	69	70
71	72	73	74	75	76	77	78	79	80
81	82	83	84	85	86	87	88	89	90
91	92	93	94	95	96	97	98	99	100

It is not until 20 that there is a number that can be divided by 2, 4 and 5 exactly. 21 is a multiple of 3, so the first number is 21, which would also leave a remainder of 1 when divided by 2, 4 or 5.

To find the second number, a similar search finds that 80 can be divided exactly by 2, 4 and 5, and that 81 can be divided exactly by 3. 81 leaves a remainder of 1 when divided by 2, 4 or 5.

17 Calculator magic

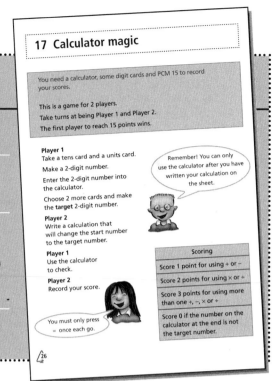

17 Calculator magic

You need a calculator, some digit cards and PCM 15 to record your scores.

This is a game for 2 players.
Take turns at being Player 1 and Player 2.
The first player to reach 15 points wins.

Player 1
Take a tens card and a units card.
Make a 2-digit number.
Enter the 2-digit number into the calculator.
Choose 2 more cards and make the **target** 2-digit number.

Player 2
Write a calculation that will change the start number to the target number.

Player 1
Use the calculator to check.

Player 2
Record your score.

Remember! You can only use the calculator after you have written your calculation on the sheet.

You must only press = once each go.

Scoring
Score 1 point for using + or −
Score 2 points for using × or ÷
Score 3 points for using more than one +, −, × or ÷
Score 0 if the number on the calculator at the end is not the target number

26

Minimum prior experience

addition of small numbers

Resources

Textbook pages 26 and 27, Hundred squares (PCM 5), PCM 15, calculators, (overhead projector, OHP calculator), 2 sets of digit cards 0–9 (PCM 7) for each pair of children (see **Differentiation**)

Key vocabulary

add, subtract, difference, total, calculate, multiply, divide, product, score, altogether

What's the problem?

A display on the calculator must be altered to a new, given, display using different operations and mental and pencil and paper methods. This encourages children to use different calculation strategies to reach a given number.

Problem solving objectives

- Choose and use appropriate number operations and appropriate ways of calculating (mental, mental with jottings, pencil and paper) to solve problems.
- Explain methods and reasoning about numbers orally and, where appropriate, in writing.
- Solve mathematical problems or puzzles, recognise simple patterns and relationships, generalise and predict. Suggest extensions by asking 'What if . . .?'

Differentiation

This activity is differentiated by the digit cards used:

More able: Cards 0–9 to make any 2-digit number.

Average: Cards 0–5 for the 'tens' pile and 0–9 for the units, to make any 2-digit number to 59.

Less able: Cards 0–9, in one pile to make the units, and 0, 1 in the other to make the tens for any number to 19.

The instructions on Textbook page 26 are the same for each group.

Introducing the problem

Check that children know how to operate the calculator for addition and subtraction. Demonstrate the game for the whole class to try, using the OHP and OHP calculator. If you don't have an OHP calculator let children follow your lead with a calculator, as you talk them through.

I have put the number 4 into the calculator display. Now, I need to change the display to 12. I can use the number buttons, add, subtract, multiply and divide and equals. How could I change the display to 12?

Give children a few moments to discuss a calculation that will do this, then ask for suggestions.

Children may suggest: 4 + 8 = 12. This would result in 1 point to the person working out the answer. However, if multiplication or division is used, e.g. 4 × 3 = 12, then that player gets 2 points. And, if more than 1 operation is used, e.g. (4 ÷ 2) × 6, the player gets 3 points. However, if the new total is wrong, then they receive no points.

Explain that the starting number is generated by taking 2 cards, randomly; then the player with the calculator takes 2 more cards to make the new target number. Their partner must write down a calculation that will change the first number to the target number, before pairs use the calculator to check.

Teacher focus for activity

All children: Children need to input the correct data into the calculator in order to reach their new total. Encourage children to use mental strategies and

jottings where they can to find a calculation that will score them most points. See **Useful mathematical information**, pages 85–86 for further information about types of calculators and their functionality.

More able: Encourage children to include multiplication and division where they can. Check whether they are using arithmetical or algebraic calculators (see **Useful mathematical information**, pages 85–86) as this can make a difference to the result.

Average: If children find the calculations difficult they may find it helpful to use a 100 square for counting.

Less able: All the calculations for addition and subtraction should, if possible, be completed by rapid recall. For multiplication and division, children may find a 100 square useful for repeated addition or subtraction, if necessary.

As children work, ask questions such as:

- *How did you work that out?*
- *Is there another way?*
- *Can you find a way to gain more points?*

Optional adult input

Work with the More able group. Encourage them to consider ways of using multiplication and division. Encourage discussions about how to calculate an answer and how to use knowledge of number relationships to score more points for a particular calculation.

Plenary

1 Invite children to share some of the problems that they set each other and how they found the solutions. Invite children to suggest alternative ways of making the target total so that they can maximise the points. For example:

Start number: 45
Target number: 12

$45 - 33 = 12$
$45 \div 5 + 3 = 12$

The second method will have 3 points.

2 Agree with children that perhaps the second method might not be the most efficient, but that it can be much more fun to try some different ways of working out the solutions to the number sentences.

Discuss which calculation methods they prefer and why. Many will prefer addition and subtraction, because of their rapid recall. Discuss how useful it is to know multiplication facts, and how these can help with working out answers to problems.

3 Play the game again, this time working in 2 teams. Choose 2 team leaders, to pick the digit cards and operate the OHT calculator, or normal calculator. Children in the team whose turn it is to reach the target number decide with the team leader which answer to input so that they maximise their points.

Development

This is an activity that can also be used for homework. If children cannot take digit cards home, they can make number circles and spin a paper clip on this.

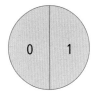

Solutions

There are no specific solutions to this activity; children create their own calculations based on the target number they drew from the piles of digit cards.

18 A street scene

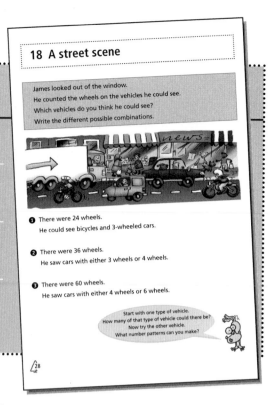

18 A street scene

James looked out of the window.
He counted the wheels on the vehicles he could see.
Which vehicles do you think he could see?
Write the different possible combinations.

❶ There were 24 wheels.
He could see bicycles and 3-wheeled cars.

❷ There were 36 wheels.
He saw cars with either 3 wheels or 4 wheels.

❸ There were 60 wheels.
He saw cars with either 4 wheels or 6 wheels.

Start with one type of vehicle.
How many of that type of vehicle could there be?
Now try the other vehicle.
What number patterns can you make?

28

Minimum prior experience

doubling; multiplication by 2 and 4

Resources

Textbook page 28, interlocking cubes, paper

Key vocabulary

times, product, multiply, multiple, pattern, calculate, mental calculation, number sentence

What's the problem?

The activity involves using multiplication and addition to investigate vehicles and their wheels. Children will multiply by 2, 3, 4 or 6 depending on their ability.

Problem solving objectives

- Choose and use appropriate number operations and appropriate ways of calculating to solve problems.
- Explain methods and reasoning about numbers orally and, where appropriate, in writing.
- Solve mathematical problems or puzzles, recognise simple patterns and relationships, generalise and predict. Suggest extensions by asking 'What if . . .?'

Differentiation

The problem on Textbook page 28 is differentiated by multiplication table and by quantity:

More able: Problem 3: 60 wheels – vehicles with 4 and 6 wheels each.

Average: Problem 2: 36 wheels – vehicles with 3 and 4 wheels each.

Less able: Problem 1: 24 wheels – vehicles with 2 and 3 wheels each.

Introducing the problem

Read the problem together. *James looked out of the window and could see all sorts of vehicles in the street.* Pause here, and ask children to suggest 2 or 3 vehicles that he might have seen, and to say how many wheels they have. *James counted the wheels. Look at how many he could see. Now I wonder which vehicles he saw.* Check that for each group children understand how many wheels there are and the types of vehicle that James saw.

Reinforce that you do not want types or makes of car, but that this is about which possible combinations of wheel numbers there are.

Ask children to discuss the problem with their partner. Explain that there are many different possible answers to the problem, so you would like them to find some answers then look for patterns.

Teacher focus for activity

All children: Children should be encouraged to use the multiplication facts they already know to deduce those that they do not. See **Useful mathematical information**, page 86 for further discussion. Encourage children to record their results systematically.

More able: Children may need help with multiplying by 6. Encourage them to consider doubling so that they can double 3s to make 6s.

Average: Children may find it helpful to double 2s to make 4s, if they do not yet have rapid recall of their 4 times table.

Less able: Children may find it helpful to write out multiples of 2s and 3s if they are unsure of these tables. They could draw a number line to 24, and mark off where the multiples of 2 and 3 are.

Ask the children questions, as they work, such as:

- *How could you work out how many there are for 2/3/4 . . . vehicles?*
- *Is the total of wheels odd or even?*
- *Which patterns can you see? How can you use those patterns to find different answers?*

Optional adult input

Work with the More able group. Encourage children to work systematically, such as looking at the patterns that emerge as the number of one of them increases and the other decreases.

Plenary

1 Ask representatives from each group to explain their results to the others. Write the results on the board, using tables as shown in the solutions. Allow the Less able group to feed back first, moving on to the Average and More able groups.

2 Consider children's responses, then ask: *What patterns did you see?*

Children may have noticed that as you increase one type of vehicle, so the other one will decrease. Ask children to explain how the multiples increase or decrease, e.g. the number of 3-wheeled vehicles goes up in 2s, while the number of 2-wheeled vehicles goes down in 3s.

3 Ask children to explain how they recorded their work. Discuss writing the results in a table, and how this can show number patterns, especially when the results are ordered.

Development

As an extension or further activity, children could take different total numbers of wheels, e.g. 20, 40 or 80, and list the different possible combinations. Alternatively, similar scenarios could be set for homework, e.g. legs on different farmyard animals. Children could also set their own questions of this kind for others to answer.

Solutions

1 For 24 wheels, both 2 and 3 divide exactly into 24. Note that the 2-wheeled vehicles have a pattern of 3s, and the 3-wheeled vehicles have a pattern of 2s.

2-wheeled vehicles	3-wheeled vehicles	Calculation
12	0	$12 \times 2 = 24$
9	2	$9 \times 2 + 2 \times 3 = 18 + 6 = 24$
6	4	$6 \times 2 + 4 \times 3 = 12 + 12 = 24$
3	6	$3 \times 2 + 6 \times 3 = 6 + 18 = 24$
0	8	$8 \times 3 = 24$

2 For 36 wheels, both 3 and 4 divide exactly into 36. Note that the 3-wheeled vehicles have a pattern of 4s, and the 4-wheeled vehicles have a pattern of 3s.

3-wheeled vehicles	4-wheeled vehicles	Calculation
12	0	$12 \times 3 = 36$
8	3	$8 \times 3 + 3 \times 4 = 24 + 12 = 36$
4	6	$4 \times 3 + 6 \times 4 = 12 + 24 = 36$
0	9	$9 \times 4 = 36$

3 For 60 wheels, both 4 and 6 divide exactly into 60. Note that the 4-wheeled vehicles have a pattern of 3s, and the 6-wheeled vehicles have a pattern of 2s. Each result gives a multiple of 12 for each type of vehicle. Both 4 and 6 are factors of 12.

4-wheeled vehicles	6-wheeled vehicles	Calculation
15	0	$15 \times 4 = 60$
12	2	$12 \times 4 + 2 \times 6 = 48 + 12 = 60$
9	4	$9 \times 4 + 4 \times 6 = 36 + 24 = 60$
6	6	$6 \times 4 + 6 \times 6 = 24 + 36 = 60$
3	8	$3 \times 4 + 8 \times 6 = 12 + 48 = 60$
0	10	$10 \times 6 = 60$

19 The blacksmith

Minimum prior experience

doubling

Resources

Textbook page 29, interlocking cubes, paper, calculators, (overhead projector and OHT calculator), base 10 materials

Key vocabulary

add, multiple of, product, double, pattern, mental calculation, jotting, pounds, pence

19 The blacksmith

❶ Farmer Fred took his horse to the blacksmith.
The horse needed 2 new shoes.
Each shoe needed 4 nails.
He paid 25p for each nail. How much did Fred pay altogether?

❷ Farmer Frank's horse needed 2 new shoes. Each shoe needed 4 nails.
He paid like this:
1 penny for the first nail.
2 pence for the second nail.
4 pence for the third nail.
8 pence for the fourth nail.
And so on.
How much did Frank pay altogether?
Who paid more, Fred or Frank?

What number pattern can you see?
What would the next number be?

❸ What if each horse needed 3 new shoes?

What's the problem?

This problem involves doubling, up to 8 or 12 times, depending on ability. Children will discover the numbers involved grow quite quickly.

Problem solving objectives

- Choose and use appropriate number operations and appropriate ways of calculating to solve problems.
- Explain methods and reasoning about numbers orally and, where appropriate, in writing.
- Solve mathematical problems or puzzles, recognise simple patterns and relationships, generalise and predict. Suggest extensions by asking 'What if . . .?'

Differentiation

More able: Problems 1, 2 and 3.

Average: Problems 1 and 2.

Less able: Problem 1.

Introducing the problem

Read the problem together. Explain that the problem is to decide which is the better way to pay. Ask children to discuss with their partner how they might solve the problem, and that you would be very interested in how they record their work.

Teacher focus for activity

All children: The problem involves understanding about doubling. To check that children understand

this, ask questions such as: *What do you need to do to solve this problem?* If appropriate, introduce the calculator and show children how to use it to double, as a means of checking their calculations.

More able: Encourage children to use mental calculation skills and jottings to work out their answers. They may find a calculator useful to check their calculations.

Average: Children should be able to work out how much 1 shoe will cost with the first method of payment, then by using doubling work out the cost of 2 shoes. Check that they understand for the second way of paying that each nail costs double the previous one. They may find number lines, 100 squares or calculators helpful for this.

Less able: Children could use base 10 materials to model the cost of the first shoe of 4 nails by the first method of paying then the second shoe. Challenge children to look at Problem 2 and work out the price of the 5th, 6th and 7th nail.

Some questions to ask as the children work:

- *How will you work this out? How will you do the doubling?*
- *Which do you think is the cheaper way to pay? Why do you think that?*

Optional adult input

Work with the Average group. Model the problem using base 10 materials for money, and show how doubling works with base 10 materials. They will need help doubling up to 128 (£1.28). Allow confident doublers to continue further if they wish.

Plenary

1 Ask children which method of paying they found cheaper. Ask:

- *Were you surprised by this?*

- *How many nails were needed for 2 shoes? (8)*

2 Demonstrate how numbers increase in size quickly when doubling.
Use an OHP calculator, and set it up to multiply by 2 each time. If you have no OHP calculator, use a normal one, and let children follow with their own calculators, to see the number grow. For some calculators it is possible to set the repeat function like this:

3 Now press zero, then 1, followed by equals, equals, equals . . . to show the growing pattern of multiplying by 2.
If the OHP calculator does not have this repeat function, input: $1 \times 2 =$, followed by $\times 2 =$, $\times 2 =$, . . .

4 Ask children to predict the next number in the series each time, so that each member of the pattern 1, 2, 4, 8, 16, 32, . . . is said before it is shown on the calculator. If children have their written responses with them, ensure that they do not look at these while the predictions are being made.
Discuss this pattern with children. They will probably be very surprised at how quickly numbers increase by doubling.

5 Now consider the more expensive way of paying and ask:

- *How much does 1 nail cost? 2 nails? 3 nails? . . .*

- *How many nails do you need altogether?*

On the board begin to draw a table like the one in **Solutions**. Invite the Less able group who have costs for 4, 5, 6 . . . nails to add these to the table. Continue with all the class until all 8 of the nail costs have been found. Cover this table with a sheet of paper so that the children can no longer see this.

6 Encourage children to explain how they set about solving this problem. Discuss how a systematic approach to this is helpful; for example, first of all work out the cost of 1 shoe of nails at 25p per nail, then the cost of 2 shoes, because this gives a quick costing for 1 method. Some children may then have worked out the cost of up to the seventh nail by the second method. Expect the More able group to have calculated the cost of up to the twelfth nail. (Problem 3)

7 Give calculators to pairs and allow them to total the cost of the second method. After doing this, emphasise that the objective of the lesson was to see which was the most expensive method and to find out how quickly numbers can increase in size by doubling.

Development

Children may like to extend the number pattern, using a calculator, to see how quickly again the pattern continues to grow. See **Useful mathematical information**, page 86 for further discussion on number patterns.

Solutions

1 First method of payment:
1 shoe will cost 4×25p which is £1.00.
So 2 shoes will cost £2.00.

2 Second method of payment:

Nails	Price
Nail 1	1p
Nail 2	2p
Nail 3	4p
Nail 4	8p
Nail 5	16p
Nail 6	32p
Nail 7	64p
Nail 8	£1.28

Total for 8 nails is £2.55 (1p + 2p + 4p + 8p . . .)
Farmer Frank paid more than Farmer Fred.

3

Nails	Price
Nail 9	£2.56
Nail 10	£5.12
Nail 11	£10.24
Nail 12	£20.48

Total for 12 nails is £3.00 or £40.95 by the first and second methods respectively.

20 Money box

Minimum prior experience

simple fractions; finding totals of coins

Resources

Textbook page 30, a selection of coins for each pair of children, to match the type of coins in their problem

Key vocabulary

part, equal parts, fraction, one whole, half, quarter, third, pound, penny, value, worth

20 Money box

① Li empties her money box.
There are 10 coins.
$\frac{1}{2}$ are 50p coins.
She also has a £1 coin, two 2p coins, a 5p coin and a 10p coin.
How much money does she have?

What is half of 10? So how many 50p coins are there in Li's box?

② Jian empties his money box.
There are 12 coins.
$\frac{1}{4}$ are 10p coins.
Another quarter are 50p coins.
He also has two £1 coins and two £2 coins.
The rest are 5p coins.
How much money does he have?

③ Zeeman has 24 coins in her money box.
$\frac{1}{3}$ are £1 coins.
$\frac{1}{3}$ are 50p coins.
She also has three 20p coins and two 10p coins.
The rest are 5p coins.
How much money does she have?

30

What's the problem?

Children use their knowledge and understanding of fractions to calculate the total value of some given coins. They calculate $\frac{1}{2}$, $\frac{1}{4}$ or $\frac{1}{3}$ of numbers, depending on their ability (see **Differentiation**).

Problem solving objectives

- Choose and use appropriate number operations and appropriate ways of calculating to solve word problems.
- Explain methods and reasoning orally and, where appropriate, in writing.
- Solve mathematical problems or puzzles, recognise simple patterns and relationships, generalise and predict. Suggest extensions by asking 'What if . . .?'

Differentiation

The problem is differentiated by the fractions of questions calculated:

More able: Problem 3: thirds (of 24)

Average: Problem 2: quarters (of 12)

Less able: Problem 1: halves (of 10)

Introducing the problem

Ask children to look at their textbook page. *You are told some information about which coins are in a money box. Now you have to work out how much money there is in total.* Remind children that they will be using their knowledge and understanding of fractions.

Check that each ability group reads their specific problem on the page.

Explain that you are interested in how children work out their answer, and in how they record their work. Ask children to decide with a partner how they will begin, then start the problem.

Teacher focus for activity

All children: Check that children remember how many of the fractional parts given make one whole. Check that children understand that one whole refers to the total number of coins in the money box, and not the value of the coins.

As children work ask questions such as:

- *What is one half . . . quarter . . . third . . . of . . .?*
- *How did you work that out?*
- *How many coins are left? How do you know that?*

More able: Ask children to calculate $\frac{1}{3}$ of 24. Agree that this is how many £1 and how many 50p coins there are.

Average: Ask children to calculate $\frac{1}{4}$ of 12. Agree that this is how many 10p and how many 50p coins there are.

Less able: Ask children to calculate $\frac{1}{2}$ of 10. Agree that this is how many 50p coins there are.

Optional adult input

Work with the Less able group. Suggest that children model the problem with coins. They may wish to share out half, like sharing half of a pile of sweets. Discuss with them how many are 'half' of the coins.

Plenary

1   Begin with Problem 1 and ask children to explain their solution and how they worked it out. Ask questions such as:

- *How many 50p coins were there?*
- *How do you know that?*
- *How did you work out $\frac{1}{2}$ of 10 coins?*

Ask a child from the group to total the coins. Encourage them to begin with the largest, and then the next largest, and so on.

2   Repeat this for Problem 2. Ask:

- *How many coins were 10p? 50p?*
- *What is the value of the 50p . . . 10p coins?*
- *How many coins were 5p? How do you know that?*
- *How did you work out $\frac{1}{4}$ of 12 coins?*

Again, when children have given their solution ask a child from the group to count out coins to demonstrate how the total was reached.

3   For Problem 3 discuss how many coins were £1 and 50p and how children worked this out. Ask:

- *How many coins were 5p?*
- *How do you know that?*
- *How much are the 5p coins worth?*
- *How did you calculate $\frac{1}{3}$ of 24 coins?*

Ask a child to put out the 24 coins and total them, beginning with the £1 coins.

4   Discuss how the fractions refer to the number of the coins, not their value. For Problem 1 ask:

- *What does 'half' mean in the problem?*
- *How much are the 50p coins worth?*
- *Is this the same value as the other 5 coins?*

Repeat this for the other problems if children are unsure about the meaning of the fractions used in these contexts.

See **Useful mathematical information** pages 86–87 for more information about finding fractions of quantities.

5   Discuss children's recording. Ask one child from each group to show their working out. Remind the class how ideas or calculations that are crossed out can help them work towards an answer, ensure they don't repeat any possibilities and give them something to check their answer against.

Development

Pose 'what if . . .?' questions if children finish, e.g. *What if half of the coins in his box were 20p coins instead of 50p coins?*

Children could try this problem for homework:

Sarah has 20 coins in her moneybox.
Half of the coins are £2 coins.
A quarter of the coins are 50p.
She also has two £1 coins and a 10p.
The rest are 20p coins.
How much money does she have in total?

Solutions

1   (10 coins)
If $\frac{1}{2}$ of the coins are 50p coins, then there are five 50p coins.
So, the total is
$(5 \times 50p) + £1 + (2 \times 2p) + 5p + 10p$
$= £2.50 + £1 + 4p + 5p + 10p = £3.69$

2   (12 coins)
If $\frac{1}{4}$ of the coins are 10p and $\frac{1}{4}$ are 50p then there are three 10p coins and three 50p coins.
The other 6 coins make up the other half. These are two £1 coins, two £2 coins, and two 5p coins.
The total is
$(3 \times 10p) + (3 \times 50p) + (2 \times £1) + (2 \times £2) + (2 \times 5p)$
$= 30p + £1.50 + £2 + £4 + 10p = £7.90$

3   (24 coins)
Each third of the coins is eight £1 coins; eight 50p coins; three 20p coins, two 10p coins and three 5p coins.
The total is
$(8 \times £1) + (8 \times 50p) + (3 \times 20p) + (2 \times 10p) + (3 \times 5p)$
$= £8 + £4 + 60p + 20p + 15p = £12.95$

Development solution

(20 coins)
$\frac{1}{2}$ (10) are £2 coins. $\frac{1}{4}$ (5) are 50p and there are two £1 coins, one 10p and two 20p coins.
The total is $(10 \times £2) + (5 \times 50p) + (2 \times £1) + 10p + 40p$
$= £20 + £2.50 + £2 + 50p = £25.00$

21 Ice cream cones

Minimum prior experience

making tables for sorting data

Resources

Textbook page 31, PCM 16, paper, coloured pencils

Key vocabulary

combination, count, sort, represent, list, chart, table, puzzle, method, justify

What's the problem?

There are 7 different ice cream flavours at the shop. Some children each buy a double scoop cone with 2 flavours of ice cream. None chooses the same combination, and all combinations are chosen. The problem is to work out how many children bought ice creams, through listing different flavours.

Problem solving objectives

- Choose and use appropriate number operations and appropriate ways of calculating to solve problems.
- Explain methods and reasoning about numbers orally and, where appropriate, in writing.
- Solve mathematical problems or puzzles, recognise simple patterns or relationships, generalise and predict. Suggest extensions by asking 'What if . . .?'

Differentiation

More able and Average: Textbook page 31.

Less able: PCM 16 has fewer combinations and a structured method of recording the choices.

Introducing the problem

Spend just a minute or two discussing ice cream stalls that have ice cream in tubs, so that you can choose which flavours you would like in your cone. (Some children may not have seen ice cream booths like these.) When children are clear about how the ice cream is sold, ask them to look at Textbook page 31 or PCM 16, and explain the problem. *Some children buy a cone with 2 different flavours of ice cream. None of the*

children have the same combination of flavours but all of the different combinations are chosen.

Check that children understand the word 'combination' in this context. If needed, provide a simpler context to ensure everyone understands. For example: *What are the combinations of 2 coloured balls you could have from this group: blue, green, yellow, red?* Allow children to list them on the board (there are 6), to understand what is involved before they begin. When children have understood the problem, ask them to discuss how they will begin to solve it and then begin.

Teacher focus for activity

All children: The first hint in the Textbook suggests thinking about how to record the different flavours. If children are not sure how to start the problem, then point them to this.

More able and Average: Encourage children to make a list or table in which they can record the combinations of flavours. Check that children are approaching this in a systematic way, so that they cover all of the possible combinations.

Less able: If children are still not sure how to begin, help them to begin to record pairs of flavours.

As children work, ask questions such as:

- *How did you decide to tackle the problem?*
- *Are all the combinations that you have found different? Is vanilla and chocolate the same as or different from chocolate and vanilla?*

Optional adult input

Work with the Average group. Help them to draw up a list or table of combinations of flavours. Children should be encouraged to work systematically, so that they are sure that they have found all the combinations.

Plenary

1 Have a table, like the one in the Solutions section, drawn on the board and covered, for later use. Ensure it is only the outline without the answers, to allow children to complete it.

2 *How did you decide to solve this problem?*
Discuss the strategies that children tried. Some will have:

- *used different colours to record each combination pictorially;*
- *written the combinations in a table;*
- *made lists of combinations in a systematic way;*
- *made lists of combinations in a random way.*

3 What problems did you have?
Discuss possible problems. Most of these will involve repeating or missing combinations while listing them. Talk about the need to follow a systematic approach to avoid repetitions or omissions.

4 Reveal the table as far as 'coffee' and invite children to help to fill it in. Check that everyone understands why there is no tick in the vanilla/vanilla box. Discuss how each child had to have 2 different flavours, so this combination would not work. Ask: *How many different combinations are there?* (10)

Reveal 'cherry' and 'orange'. Using column then row, ask:

- *Why is there no tick in the vanilla/chocolate box?*
- *Why are there no ticks at all in the orange row? Does this mean that nobody had a combination including orange?*
- *So, can you explain why there is only 1 tick in the cherry row?*

Remind children, if necessary, that a vanilla/chocolate combination is the same as a chocolate/vanilla one. If children are unsure about this, draw a double cone, so that they can see that these are the same.

5 Ask children which strategy for recording they thought was best. Talk about working systematically, so that all the possibilities are included, and how a table can ensure that nothing is missed.

Development

Ask children to think of 2 more flavours to add to the list. Ask: *What if there were 9 different flavours to choose from? How many different combinations would there be?* (36)

Solutions

A simple table will show the combinations at a glance. With 5 flavours there are 10 combinations. With 7 flavours there are 21 combinations, and so 21 children bought ice creams. Some children may have seen other tables presented like this, such as sports fixtures in newspapers or on school notice boards.

	Vanilla	Chocolate	Raspberry	Strawberry	Coffee	Cherry	Orange
Vanilla		✓	✓	✓	✓	✓	✓
Chocolate			✓	✓	✓	✓	✓
Raspberry				✓	✓	✓	✓
Strawberry					✓	✓	✓
Coffee						✓	✓
Cherry							✓
Orange							

These can then be totalled, to give the number of children who bought an ice cream.

Note that if this method of recording is used, then the results form a visual pattern and it is easy to check. There is no doubling of flavours, such as vanilla and chocolate, and chocolate and vanilla, nor is there doubling of the same flavour. See **Useful mathematical information**, page 87 for further discussion about the use of tables as an aid in problem solving activities.

22 Pick up sticks

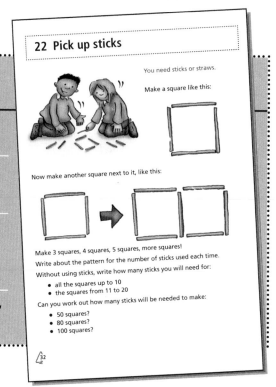

22 Pick up sticks

You need sticks or straws.

Make a square like this:

Now make another square next to it, like this:

Make 3 squares, 4 squares, 5 squares, more squares!

Write about the pattern for the number of sticks used each time.

Without using sticks, write how many sticks you will need for:
- all the squares up to 10
- the squares from 11 to 20

Can you work out how many sticks will be needed to make:
- 50 squares?
- 80 squares?
- 100 squares?

32

Minimum prior experience

counting and counting patterns in 2s, 3s and 4s

Resources

Textbook page 32, paper for recording, Cuisenaire rods all of the same size, or counting sticks, pencils or cut up straws

Key vocabulary

number, count, how many . . .?, relationship, puzzle, pattern, total, square, predict, make a statement

What's the problem?

Children are asked to make growing square and triangular patterns using practical resources, then to spot the number pattern.

Problem solving objectives

- Choose and use appropriate number operations and appropriate ways of calculating to solve problems.
- Explain methods and reasoning about numbers orally and, where appropriate, in writing.
- Solve mathematical problems or puzzles, recognise simple patterns and relationships, generalise and predict. Suggest extensions by asking 'What if . . .?'

Differentiation

The problem on page 32 of the pupil Textbook is differentiated by outcome.

Introducing the problem

Draw a square that looks as though it is made from sticks or straws.

Imagine that I made this square from some sticks. How many sticks did I use? Now suppose I put some more sticks on to the square so that now there are 2 squares. How many sticks did I need for this?

Explain that the problem is to work out how many sticks are needed for 3, 4, 5 . . . squares and to try to spot a number pattern.

Remind children that they can use resources to make the squares and that they may find it helpful to draw what they make on paper. Ask them to record their thinking.

Teacher focus for activity

All children: Encourage children to write down how many sticks are used for each new square and to show the total for their square patterns.

More able: Children should quickly move from using resources to drawing on paper, to record the number of sticks each time. Challenge children to find how many sticks are needed for 50 . . . 80 . . . 100 squares.

Average: Encourage children to move from using resources to drawing on paper.

Less able: Children will probably find it easier to use the sticks each time to make the next square initially, but should soon be able to move to drawing on paper.

Ask questions, as children work:

- *How many sticks do you need for 1/2/3 . . . squares? So how many do you think you need for the next size of square?*
- *Which number pattern can you see? Can you explain this to me?*

Optional adult input

Work with the Less able group. Help them to record their findings. See if any children can begin to predict the number of sticks needed for future squares and then try this out to see if their predictions are correct.

Plenary

1 Invite various children to demonstrate how the squares grow, by drawing them on the board. Make a simple table:

Number of squares	Number of sticks
1	4
2	7
3	10
4	13
5	16
6	19
7	22
8	25
9	28
10	31

2 Ask children to spot any patterns.

They should notice that the number pattern increases by 3 each time from the starting point of 4. Ask:

- *How many sticks do you think we shall need for 11 squares? 12? 13 . . .?*

- *How did you work this out?*

Complete the table for squares 11 to 20.

Number of squares	Number of sticks
11	34
12	37
13	40
14	43
15	46
16	49
17	52
18	55
19	58
20	61

3 Ask children to say the number pattern, beginning with 4, and counting on 3 each time.

Development

On the board draw this triangle pattern and ask:

- *How many sticks for the first triangle? Second?*

- *How many do you think there will be for the third? Fourth . . .?*

- *How did you work that out?*

Invite children to say the counting pattern, this time starting on 3, and counting on 2 each time: 3, 5, 7, 9 . . .

Here is the pattern for the triangles:

Number of triangles	Number of sticks
1	3
2	5
3	7
4	9
5	11
6	13
7	15
8	17
9	19
10	21

With children's help, write this pattern on the board, and invite children to predict the eleventh, twelfth . . . triangle pattern of sticks. See **Useful mathematical information**, page 87 for further information on number patterns.

Solutions

See the table in **Plenary**. If children have attempted 50, 80 or 100 squares, the solutions are as follows:

50 squares: $4 + (49 \times 3)$
$$= 147 + 4$$
$$= 151$$
80 squares: $4 + (79 \times 3)$
$$= 4 + 237$$
$$= 241$$
100 squares: $4 + (99 \times 3)$
$$= 4 + 297$$
$$= 301$$

23 Sticky squares

23 Sticky squares

You need sticks or straws.

Make a square like this:
Call it: '1'.

Problem 1

Add sticks to make an 'L' shape, like this:
Call it '2'.

How many sticks does shape '2' use?

Add more sticks to make a larger 'L'.
Call it '3'.

How many sticks does shape '3' use?

Can you find a pattern?

Predict how many sticks you will need for shape '5'.

Problem 2

Start with the first square '1'.

Add sticks to make a cross shape, like this:
Call it '2'.

Make the cross larger by adding more sticks to each side. Call it '3'.

Now make shape '4' and shape '5'.

How many sticks do you need for each shape?
What number pattern can you see?

Predict how many sticks you will need for shape '10'.

33

What's the problem?

Children are asked to make growing square patterns, where the size of the pattern increases each time. Children are asked to spot the number pattern, and predict totals for future patterns.

Problem solving objectives

● Choose and use appropriate number operations and appropriate ways of calculating to solve problems.

● Explain methods and reasoning about numbers orally and, where appropriate, in writing.

● Solve mathematical problems or puzzles, recognise simple patterns and relationships, generalise and predict. Suggest extensions by asking 'What if . . .?'

Differentiation

The activity on Textbook page 33 is differentiated by outcome. Children start with Problem 1 and some may move on to Problem 2.

Introducing the problem

Introduce Problem 1. Draw a square, as if it is made from sticks and call this '1'. Now create an 'L' shape, made by adding 2 squares (1 at each side of the original square) and call it '2'.

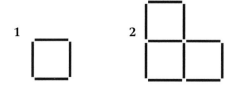

How many sticks do you need to make shape '1'? And how many sticks to make shape '2'?

Explain that you would like children to make shapes 3, 4, 5 . . . and see if they can spot a number pattern for how many sticks are needed.

Ask children to record what they do, and to begin Problem 1 straight away.

Teacher focus for activity

All children: Encourage children to write down how many sticks are used for each new shape and to show the total for their patterns.

More able: Children should quickly move from using resources to drawing on paper, to record the number of sticks each time.

Average: Encourage children to move from using resources to drawing on paper.

Less able: Children may find it easier to use the sticks each time to make the next shape. Ask them to record how many sticks they used each time on paper.

Ask questions, as the children work:

● *How many sticks do you need for this size of cross? So how many do you think you need for the next size of cross?*

● *What number pattern can you see? Can you explain this to me?*

Optional adult input

Work with the Less able group. Help them to record what they do.

66

See if children can begin to predict the number of sticks needed for future crosses. Try to ensure that their predictions are based on previous patterns or knowledge.

Plenary

1   Invite various children to draw the stick patterns on the board and to make a table, like the one below, to show how many sticks. Ask questions, such as:

● *How many sticks did the first square need?*

● *How many sticks in the first 'L'? And the second? And the third?*

● *What pattern is there?*

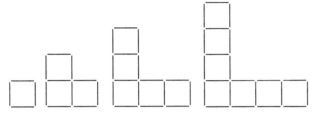

Pattern	Number of sticks
1	4
2	10
3	16
4	22

The pattern grows by 6 each time from 4, because each arm of the 'L' needs another 3 sticks to make the next square.

2   Invite children to draw the crosses created for Problem 2. See if they can spot a pattern for total number of sticks used. Encourage children to say the pattern with you.

Shape	Number of sticks
1	4
2	16
3	28
4	40
5	52

Each shape needs 12 more sticks than the previous one, because each of the 4 arms of the pattern needs 3 further sticks.

3   Invite children to predict what the next one would be, and the next, and each time ask a child to draw the pattern on the board so that children can see if they were correct. Children should notice that the pattern increases by 12 each time. Ask:

● *Why does the pattern increase by 12 each time?*

If children are not sure about this, ask them how much 1 arm of the cross shape increases each time, and then how much 4 arms will increase.

4   Say the pattern together: 4, 16, 28, 40, 52, 64, 76, 88, 100 . . .

5   Invite various children to talk about how they recorded their work. Ask the More able group to discuss how they quickly moved to calculating the number of sticks needed and then checking with a drawing, instead of just building on to each larger shape.

Development

A further growing patterns problem is included in Useful mathematical information, pages 87–88. It can be used in class or set for homework. There is also further discussion on number patterns.

Solutions

See tables in **Plenary**. Problem 1 increases by 6 sticks each time and Problem 2 by 12 sticks each time.

24 Squares and triangles

Minimum prior experience

properties of squares and right-angled triangles

Resources

Textbook page 34, PCM 17, paper, glue, squared paper, scissors, envelopes, (A3 enlargement of PCM 17 with the 'L' shapes cut out, mirrors)

Key vocabulary

square, triangle, right-angled triangle, turn, reflect, rotate, fit, justify, puzzle, how did you work it out?

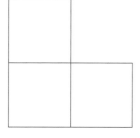

24 Squares and triangles

You need PCM 17 with the ▊▊ shapes cut out.

Remove a right-angled triangle from one of your 'L' shapes by cutting off half a square.

Find different ways of doing this so you get a new shape each time. Repeat, cutting off 2 right-angled triangles each time. Draw your shapes on squared paper.

Check, by turning, that none of your shapes are the same.

Keep your shapes safe. You will need them for another puzzle.

34

What's the problem?

Starting from an 'L' shape made with 3 squares, the children are asked to cut off a right-angled triangle and to find different shapes by doing this. Then they are asked to cut off 2 right-angled triangles to make further different shapes. They need to ensure that the shapes are not the same, by turning them over and rotating them.

Problem solving objectives

- Solve mathematical problems or puzzles, recognise simple patterns or relationships, generalise and predict. Suggest extensions by asking 'What if . . .?' or 'What could I try next?'
- Explain methods and reasoning orally and, where appropriate, in writing.

Differentiation

The activity on Textbook page 34 is for the whole class and is differentiated by outcome.

Introducing the problem

On the board draw an 'L' shape from squares, like this:

Explain first of all that they have to make different shapes from a 3-square 'L' shape like this one, by cutting off a right-angled triangle.

Then, the next part of the puzzle is to cut off 2 right-angled triangles from 3-square 'L' shapes, this time making different shapes altogether.

Make sure that all children understand the 2 stages to the problem.

Focus on 'right-angled triangle' if children have not covered this yet. Explain that cutting a square diagonally in half will create a right-angled triangle. Use folded paper, square 2-D shapes or geo-strips to reinforce or teach what a right angle is. Ensure that children understand what a right-angled triangle is, so that they don't cut off another kind of triangle.

Provide copies of PCM 17, which has the 'L' shapes ready for cutting out. Also provide some squared paper, so that children can draw the shapes that they make as a record.

Teacher focus for activity

All children: If children are unsure about what to do, demonstrate cutting a right-angled triangle from a square (see Plenary).

More able and Average: Encourage children to check by turning that they have made a unique shape each time, rather than the same shape with a different orientation. Children may want to use mirrors to check that they have not made a reflected shape.

Less able: Ask children to check that their new shape is unique by placing it on top of the other shapes that they have made, and rotating it, then turning it over, to check that there is not another shape the same with a different orientation.

As children work ask questions, such as:

- *Is this a new shape? How do you know?*
- *How can you check that you do not have 2 shapes the same?*

Optional adult input

Work with the Average group. Help them to check that each shape they make is unique, and ensure that they progress from stage 1 of cutting off 1 right-angled triangle, to cutting off 2 triangles.

Plenary

1 Invite a child to take 1 of the enlarged 'L' shapes and to cut off a right-angled triangle so that it looks like one of their solutions. Ask children how many different shapes can be created in this way. Allow children to come forward with what they believe to be a different shape, and invite comments from others about how the shape is the same. Repeat this until there are 3 different shapes made by cutting off one right angle. Ask:

- *How can we tell if these shapes are the same or different from each other?*

Invite a child to test by rotating; then turning it over. See **Useful mathematical information**, page 88 for further discussion on reflective and rotational symmetry.

2 Discuss how each of these shapes is different from one another. Encourage children to use the mathematical language of shape and space to explain this.

They may say:

- When you cut off a triangle, you think you have a different shape, but when you turn it over, it's the same.
- Turning the shape over and rotating it can make it look different, but actually, it's the same.

3 Now repeat this for the shapes that have 2 right-angled triangles cut off. Ask children to confirm whether or not they believe that each shape is unique as soon as it has been cut out. Invite a child to rotate and turn over the shape to check. Continue until you have found the 5 different shapes that exist.

4 Invite different children to explain how they went about the task, and how they ensured that each of their shapes was different.

Some children may show how shapes can be placed one on the other, then one of them rotated or turned over to check. Others may demonstrate how they checked, by using a mirror.

5 Finally, pin all of the enlarged shapes onto the board, numbered 1 to 8, and ask a child to come out and choose 1 of the shapes. Without telling other children which shape has been chosen, the child describes the shape. The others try to guess which shape is being described. Encourage the use of appropriate mathematical language for this such as: diagonal, square, right-angled triangle, edge, middle, corner, point, half turn, quarter turn.

6 At the end of the lesson, ask the children to place their loose cut out shapes safely inside an envelope, as they will need these pieces for Lesson 26.

Development

Lesson 26 will use the shapes produced in this activity. Children could develop their mathematical vocabulary by describing (orally and written) other shapes by their properties for others to work out.

Solutions

See **Plenary** for diagrams. There are a total of 8 different shapes: 3 from cutting off 1 right-angled triangle, and 5 from cutting off 2.

25 Fold a shape

Minimum prior experience

counting sequences; doubling; 2-D shapes

Resources

Textbook page 35, A5 or A6 sheets of paper, sugar paper for recording, glue

Key vocabulary

number, count, fold, quadrilateral, square, rectangle, triangle, pentagon, hexagon, heptagon, octagon, nonagon, regular, irregular, (vertex, vertices, side)

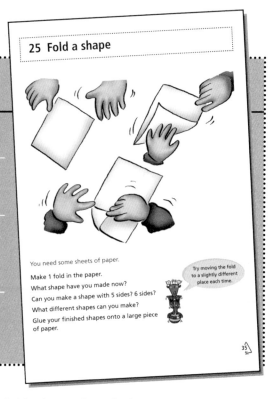

25 Fold a shape

You need some sheets of paper.

Make 1 fold in the paper.

What shape have you made now?

Can you make a shape with 5 sides? 6 sides?

What different shapes can you make?

Glue your finished shapes onto a large piece of paper.

Try moving the fold to a slightly different place each time.

35

What's the problem?

The activity involves folding a piece of paper to make shapes with different numbers of sides. Children will reinforce and learn new 2-D shape names, as well as thinking about the effect of modifying shapes in different ways.

Problem solving objectives

- Solve mathematical problems or puzzles, recognise simple patterns and relationships, generalise and predict. Suggest extensions by asking 'What if . . .?'

- Investigate a general statement about familiar numbers or shapes by finding examples that satisfy it.

Differentiation

The activity on Textbook page 35 is for the whole class and is differentiated by outcome.

Introducing the problem

Pin up a sheet of A4 paper and ask:

- *How many sides does this have?*
- *And how many angles?*
- *What is it called?* (rectangle)
- *Can anyone think of any other 4-sided shapes?* (square)

If children do not already know the word, teach them that shapes with 4 sides, including squares and rectangles are known as 'quadrilaterals'. You may wish to elaborate about 'quad' – from the Latin for 4 – through words such as:

'quadruple' (× 4), 'quadrangle' (open space surrounded by 4 sides in a building) or 'quadraphonic' (music system with 4 speakers).

- *Can you think of a way to fold this sheet of paper so that you can make a different flat shape?*

Children may suggest, for example, folding up 1 end to make a square.

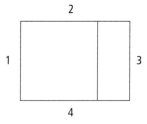

Ask children to investigate this further. Explain that you would like them to investigate what 2-D shapes they can make, including those with more than 4 sides, by making just 1 fold in a sheet of A4 paper.

Suggest that they mount each folded piece of paper on to a large sheet of sugar paper, and number the sides of their shape.

Ask them to begin the investigation straight away.

Teacher focus for activity

All children: Encourage children to search for different ways of making 1 fold. Check that children realise that the fold can cause an overlap, like this, in order to create more sides and new shapes. Ensure that they count the number of sides correctly and begin to recall the names of different-sided shapes.

More able: Encourage children to work systematically, so that they find how to fold the paper to make 4, 5, 6 or more-sided shapes, in order.

Average and Less able: Children may work randomly, trying different ways of folding the paper. Encourage them to look at each shape that they make and to consider how else they could fold the paper to make a different number of sides.

As children work, ask questions such as:

- *What do you think is the least number of sides you can make? (4)*
- *Have you found the most, do you think? (9)*

Optional adult input

Work with the More able group. Encourage them to predict how they can create different shapes by folding different parts of the paper. Challenge them to find out the names of a 7- or a 9-sided shape, if they manage to create one.

Plenary

1   Invite various children to demonstrate how they made each shape. Children can fold fresh sheets of paper to demonstrate, and it is likely that there will be different solutions for each number of sides.

2   Ask:

- *What is the name of this shape?*

Children should know the names for some of their shapes. The following table gives shape names.

Sides	Name
4	quadrilateral
5	pentagon
6	hexagon
7	heptagon
8	octagon
9	nonagon

Children of this age may know some of these shape names. Decide if they will enjoy learning and using the others. More shape names can be found in **Useful mathematical information,** page 88.

3   Ask questions such as:

- *Do all pentagons/hexagons . . . look like this?*
- *Is this a regular shape? How do you know?*

Emphasise that these are **irregular** shapes because they do not have sides of equal length (apart from the square, which is regular).

4   Discuss how children worked to find their shapes. They may suggest that they:

- tried different folds to see what happened;
- worked systematically, finding shapes with 4, 5, then 6 . . . sides.

Discuss their way of working and what they notice about the shapes they made. They may notice that by moving the placing of the fold slightly they will increase or decrease the number of sides. For example, in the solutions, the same sort of fold, but in a slightly different place, produced 6, 7, 8 and 9 sides.

5   Finish with a simple quiz about shape names, asking questions such as:

- *Which shape has 1 more than 5 sides?*
- *Which shape has 7 vertices?*
- *Did you make any shapes that had no right angles?*
- *Which shapes did you make which had 2/3/4 right angles?*
- *Why is this shape irregular?*

Development

For homework, or as an extension to this lesson, children may like to try 2 folds, and find out the different kinds of triangles they can make. They may also like to see if it is possible to create more than 9 sides with 2 folds, and discover what names these irregular shapes have (see **Useful mathematical information,** page 88).

Congratulate the children on their work. Their completed sheets could be used as a wall display, with the shape names added.

Solutions

These are some of the possible solutions. The children will probably find others, too!

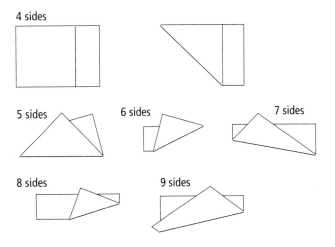

26 Make that shape

You need these shapes that you made for Lesson 24 Squares and triangles.

Which shapes can you use to cover each shape on page 37?

36

Minimum prior experience

Lesson 24

Resources

Textbook pages 36 and 37, PCM 18, A3 enlargement of PCM 18, shapes that children made for Lesson 24, squared paper, plain paper, A3-enlarged shapes made for Lesson 24 from PCM 17, Blu-Tack

Key vocabulary

square, triangle, right-angled triangle, turn, flip, fit, beside, between, diagonal, sideways, above, below

What's the problem?

Using shapes (made during Lesson 24, or made from PCM 17 if Lesson 24 not covered), children find ways of fitting some of them together in order to make new shapes. Shapes can be flipped or rotated.

Problem solving objectives

- Solve mathematical problems or puzzles, recognise simple patterns or relationships, generalise and predict. Suggest extensions by asking 'What if . . .?'

Differentiation

The activity on Textbook pages 36 and 37 is for the whole class and is differentiated by outcome.

Introducing the problem

Remind children of the shapes that they made for Lesson 24. Ask them to look at their Textbook page and explain: *Find which cut out shapes fit together to cover the larger ones.*

Explain to children that they may find more than 1 way of covering the shapes. They can use the outlines on Textbook page 37 to put their shapes on, and then record what they have found out by drawing on PCM 18.

Children may flip or rotate their shapes in order to solve the puzzles.

Teacher focus for activity

All children: Check that children understand that they can flip or rotate their pieces in order to find the solution to covering the shapes. See **Useful mathematical information**, page 88 for further detail on reflective and rotational symmetry.

More able and Average: Children may find it helpful to keep sketches of what they have tried. They will find squared paper useful for recording this.

Less able: Children will be supported by placing their shapes on the copies, linking them together to create combinations that fill the area. They could record their attempts by sketching onto squared paper, or they may find it helpful to draw around their shapes to record combinations that they have tried. They will find plain paper useful for this.

Ask questions as children work, such as:

- *How did you make that shape?*
- *What shapes will you try for this one? Why do you think that will work?*

Optional adult input

Work with the Less able group. Help them to record their attempts. Remind them about looking at the small shapes, and suggest fitting them around the corners and sides first, to ensure all the possible squares are being filled. They should discuss what fitted and what did not fit.

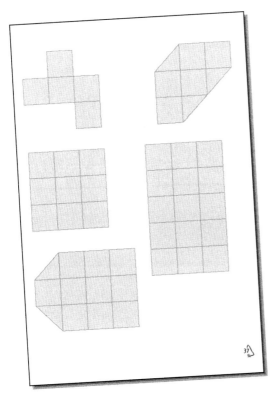

Plenary

1   Pin the enlarged PCM 18 onto the board. Invite children from each group to use the enlarged pieces and to place them onto the first outline on the enlarged PCM. Ask:

● *How did you work out which pieces to put on this outline?*

● *Did anyone find another solution to this?*

● *What else did you try? Why did it not fit?*

2   Repeat this for the other shapes, giving children time to check what they have done, and to check whether they have found any other solutions.

Ask:

● *What did you and your partner decide to do in order to solve the problem?*

● *How did you record what you tried? How did this help you?*

3   Invite some children from each ability group to show how they recorded their trials. Discuss how this can help them to spot a winning solution by seeing how the pieces fit together.

Some children may have counted how many whole squares and right-angled triangles they needed to cover the outlines. Discuss how this can be a helpful strategy because it gives some indication of which combinations of pieces will not work. Remind children that some of the pieces have just 1 right-angled triangle cut off, so that these pieces have 2 squares each. The others have 2 right-angled triangles cut off, so that these have 1 square and 2 half squares each.

4   Discuss how the shapes fitted together, encouraging children to use the language of shape and space appropriately as they make their explanations (see **Key vocabulary**). Other children may follow what is said by making the moves and turns with their shapes.

Development

Ask children to make up some more outlines using some or all of their 8 pieces as a guide. They should also make an 'answer sheet' showing how they filled the outlines. Children could swap their outline sheets to fill with the pieces.

Solutions

The following shows 1 solution for each of the outline shapes. The children may, of course, find some different solutions, particularly for the coverage of the rectangle, which could be a horizontal or vertical flip of this solution, or a rotation through 180°.

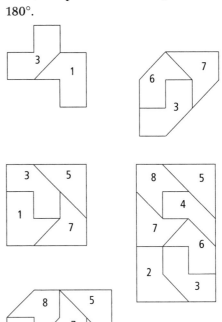

based on:

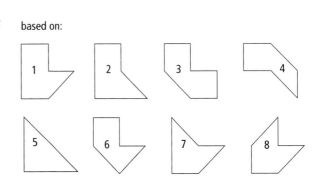

27 Jamie's walk

Minimum prior experience

programming Roamer or using Logo

Resources

Textbook pages 38 and 39, PCM 19, A3 enlargement of PCM 19, coloured pencils

Key vocabulary

forward, back, turn, left, right, plot, whole turn, half turn, quarter turn, clockwise, anti-clockwise, right angle

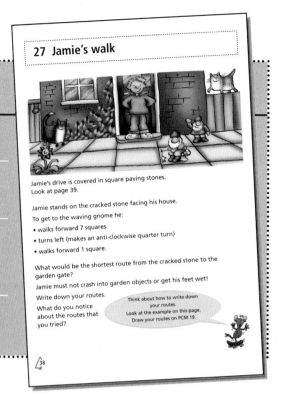

27 Jamie's walk

Jamie's drive is covered in square paving stones. Look at page 39.

Jamie stands on the cracked stone facing his house. To get to the waving gnome he:
- walks forward 7 squares
- turns left (makes an anti-clockwise quarter turn)
- walks forward 1 square.

What would be the shortest route from the cracked stone to the garden gate?

Jamie must not crash into garden objects or get his feet wet!

Write down your routes.

What do you notice about the routes that you tried?

Think about how to write down your routes. Look at the example on this page. Draw your routes on PCM 19.

38

What's the problem?

This puzzle involves plotting a route using Logo-type language to write down the route.

It develops describing positions and directions, allowing children to think of different possible routes and numbers of moves.

Problem solving objectives

- Solve mathematical problems or puzzles, recognise simple patterns or relationships, generalise and predict. Suggest extensions by asking 'What if . . .?'

Differentiation

The activity on Textbook pages 38 and 39 is for the whole class and is differentiated by outcome and support given.

Introducing the problem

Ask children to look at the Textbook page, and read the problem together. Remind children: You are asked to find the shortest route. *You may not go through the pond or crash into other garden objects.*

Explain key vocabulary, e.g. clockwise/anti-clockwise, by asking children to stand up and turn each way. Use a clock face to remind them. Incorporate quarter/half/whole turn and then ask individuals to try to follow instructions, with others watching and checking.

Provide copies of PCM 19 for children to record their routes. They may need more than 1 copy of this. They can record more than 1 route on a sheet if they use coloured crayons to mark the route.

Invite children to discuss how they will solve the problem with their partner. They should begin straight away.

Teacher focus for activity

All children: Check that children know which is left and which is right and that they understand that Jamie has to turn left or right before moving forward in a new direction.

More able and Average: Encourage children to 'say' their route to each other, for their partner to follow.

Less able: When children have drawn in a route, ask them to say the route with you, so that you can check that they know and understand the vocabulary of position, direction and movement.

Ask questions as the children work, such as:
- *Which do you think is the shortest route?*
- *Which directions would you write?*
- *How could you make your route longer/shorter?*

Optional adult input

Work with the Less able group. Check that they can use the vocabulary of position, direction and movement appropriately (see **Key vocabulary**). Move the hands on a clock to check clockwise/anti-clockwise and support children's understanding of these phrases.

Plenary

1 Invite various children to show 1 of their shortest routes by drawing it on the A3 PCM enlargement that is pinned to the board. Each route could be described by a child, with another child who has not worked with them, following it on the board with their finger. As they read it, the rest of the class could check that the route is correctly described and the child is following correctly. Each route could be shown with a different coloured felt pen and several enlarged sheets could be used. Ask:

● *How many squares are visited in the shortest routes?*

● *What is the same about all of these routes?*

2 Encourage the children to discuss how the routes always move forward, and never include a backward move.

3 Now, use a fresh enlarged PCM and invite a child to draw a route that is longer. This will involve some moves backwards. Ask:

● *Why is this longer?*

● *How did you describe it?*

4 Invite various children to describe another route on the board, using the appropriate vocabulary to describe movement and direction (see **Key vocabulary**).

Development

A new problem could be set in a lesson or for homework where children use PCM 19 to record their work. Examples include:

1 Jamie visits the flowerpot and the pond on the way to the cracked stone from the garden gate.

2 Jamie goes from the bush to the front door, going around the flowerbed once on the way.

3 Jamie goes from the garden gate to the front door, visiting all the parts where plants are growing on the way.

All of these could be carried out, trying to gain the shortest route and trying different directions in differing sequences. See **Useful mathematical information**, page 88 for further suggestions for using Logo.

Solutions

Provided that all of the moves are 'forwards' so that there is no backtracking, then to cover any of the shortest routes involves visiting 14 squares. The diagram below shows 3 of the many possible routes.

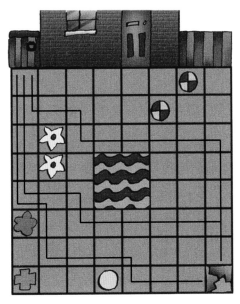

Key

⊕ **garden gnome**

✚ **dustbin**

✺ **flower bed**

✿ **bush**

〰 **pond**

○ **flowerpot**

▨ **cracked stone**

28 A weighty problem

Minimum prior experience

weighing in grams and kilograms

Resources

Textbook page 40, scales, balances, weights, class maths books, paper for recording, calculators, (overhead projector, OHP calculator)

Key vocabulary

balances, weigh, kilogram (kg), half kilogram, gram (g), balance, scales, calculate, mental calculation, estimate, how did you work it out?, investigate

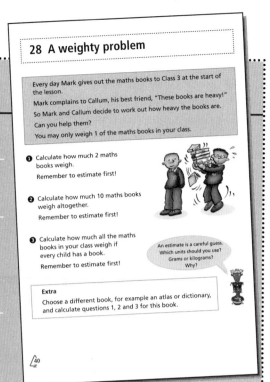

28 A weighty problem

Every day Mark gives out the maths books to Class 3 at the start of the lesson.

Mark complains to Callum, his best friend, "These books are heavy!"

So Mark and Callum decide to work out how heavy the books are.

Can you help them?

You may only weigh 1 of the maths books in your class.

❶ Calculate how much 2 maths books weigh.
Remember to estimate first!

❷ Calculate how much 10 maths books weigh altogether.
Remember to estimate first!

❸ Calculate how much all the maths books in your class weigh if every child has a book.
Remember to estimate first!

An estimate is a careful guess. Which units should you use? Grams or kilograms? Why?

Extra
Choose a different book, for example an atlas or dictionary, and calculate questions 1, 2 and 3 for this book.

40

What's the problem?

By weighing one of the class maths books, the children calculate the weight of more books. They will use estimating and rounding skills.

Problem solving objectives

- Choose and use appropriate number operations and ways of calculating to solve problems.
- Explain methods and reasoning about numbers orally and in writing.
- Solve mathematical problems or puzzles, recognise simple patterns and relationships, generalise and predict. Suggest extensions by asking 'What if . . .?'
- Solve word problems involving numbers in 'real life', money and measures, using 1 or more steps. Explain how the problem was solved.

Differentiation

The activity on Textbook page 40 is differentiated as follows:

More able: Problem 3: total weight of all the books.

Average: Problem 2: weight of 10 books.

Less able: Problem1: weight of 2 books..

Introducing the problem

If possible find books that have a 'convenient' weight, such as a weight that is a multiple of 10. Make a pile of books, with enough for 1 for everyone in the class.

Invite a child to pick up some of the maths books and describe how heavy they feel. *Imagine carrying all these books at once to give them out so that everyone in the class has a book. Your problem is to work out how much some books weigh, but you will only be allowed to weigh 1 book.*

Clarify with each group how many books children must consider. Discuss 'estimating' and how it is a 'sensible' or 'careful' guess, based on what they already know. Remind them that it doesn't matter if the estimate is inaccurate, it is there to give them a guide to check their answer against. Ask children to talk with their partner about how they will solve the problem. Children should start the problem straight away.

Teacher focus for activity

All children: Discuss with children the units that they will use, and why they have chosen these. Encourage children to make an estimate first, based upon picking up 1 book.

More able: Discuss how they will make their calculation of the total weight. Check that they know how many grams in a kilogram and that they can translate from grams to kilograms. Encourage children to use a rounding method first, then check with a calculator.

Average: Discuss how they will make their calculation of the total weight. Check that they know how many grams in a kilogram and that they can translate from grams to kilograms. Suggest that they multiply the hundreds of grams by 10, and discuss how this can be converted into kilograms; then the tens by 10, and so on.

Less able: Check that children understand how to weigh 1 book with reasonable accuracy. In order to calculate the weight of 2 books, they may want to double each digit separately, then re-combine.

Ask children questions as they work, such as:
- *How much do you estimate 1 book will weigh?*
- *So, how much do you estimate 2/10/all the books weigh?*
- *How will you work out how much 2/10/all the books weigh?*

Optional adult input

Work with the More able group. Help them to find a method of calculating the weight of all the books.

Plenary

1 Invite those who tried Problem 1 to discuss how they decided to solve the problem. Ask questions such as:
   - *How heavy was 1 book?*
   - *So how did you work out the weight of 2 books?*

   Suggestions for a book weighing, e.g. 276 g, could include:
   - weighing the book using the gram weights and it was about 200, and 50, and 20 and about 5;
   - doubling each of the weights to 400, and a 100, and 40 and a 10;
   - adding these together.

   This is a perfectly acceptable method. Children who used this method may have found it useful to use the weights, so that they doubled each weight in front of them.

2 Now invite those who worked on Problem 2 to explain how they solved the problem. Children may have:
   - weighed 1 book;
   - put the weights that they used in front of them, and calculated each 1 separately, such as:
     10×200 g $+ 10 \times 70$ g $+ 10 \times 5$ g

Again, this is a perfectly acceptable method.

NB: If children have weighed 1 book and simply added '0' to the end for multiplying by 10, discuss this with them and check that they understand what happens if 75 g is multiplied by 10. Now ask what happens if 1.5 kg is multiplied by 10 to check their understanding.

3 Ask those who attempted Problem 3 to explain how they worked out the total weight of enough books for the whole class. Methods may include:
   - working out the weight of 10, then adding multiples of these, and single books;
   - rounding up the starting number. So, for 276 g they could round this to 280 g and adjust by 4 g for each book at the end;
   - check with a calculator.

4 Use the OHP calculator, or a normal calculator with children following with theirs, to show how the calculation could be made. For example, for books weighing 276 g each, and for a class of 32 children the calculation would be:
   $32 \times 276 = 8832$

   Discuss what 8832 g means: 8 kilograms and 832 grams. Reinforce that 1000 g = 1 kg.

Development

When children are confident with the methods that they have seen, they could:
- repeat the activity for another set of books, this time trying a different method of calculation;
- use calculators and practise estimating with different numbers to calculate the weight of maths books for 15 or 20 books, or even 2 classes.

See **Useful mathematical information**, page 88 for a discussion on the difference between mass and weight.

Solutions

Solutions will vary according to the weight of the original book. Check children's methods and working out, both orally in their explanation, and written in their books.

29 Tennis matches

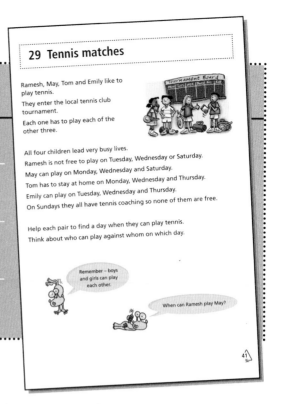

29 Tennis matches

Ramesh, May, Tom and Emily like to play tennis.

They enter the local tennis club tournament.

Each one has to play each of the other three.

All four children lead very busy lives.
Ramesh is not free to play on Tuesday, Wednesday or Saturday.
May can play on Monday, Wednesday and Saturday.
Tom has to stay at home on Monday, Wednesday and Thursday.
Emily can play on Tuesday, Wednesday and Thursday.
On Sundays they all have tennis coaching so none of them are free.

Help each pair to find a day when they can play tennis.
Think about who can play against whom on which day.

Remember – boys and girls can play each other.

When can Ramesh play May?

41

Minimum prior experience

days of the week; making tables and lists

Resources

Textbook page 41, PCM 20, paper

Key vocabulary

time, days of the week, timetable, count, sort, data, represent, table, method

What's the problem?

Four children like to play tennis, but they lead such busy lives that they need help with finding when they are all free. The problem is to work out when they can play. Children will be listing possible outcomes, sorting data and creating and interpreting tables.

Problem solving objectives

- Solve mathematical problems or puzzles, recognise and explain patterns and relationships, generalise and predict. Suggest extensions by asking 'What if . . .?'

- Explain methods of calculation and reasoning about numbers orally and, where appropriate, in writing.

- Solve word problems involving numbers in 'real life', money and measures, using 1 or more steps. Explain how the problem was solved.

Differentiation

More able: Textbook page 41.

Average: Textbook page 41. Give children the 6 questions at the bottom of PCM 20 to support their reasoning.

Less able: PCM 20 provides the same problem with a recording table for support.

Introducing the problem

Ask children to look at the problem on Textbook page 41 or PCM 20. Read it through with them, and explain what you want them to do. *Your problem is to work out when each pair of children could play their tennis match.*

Explain that you are particularly interested in how children go about solving this problem and how they record what they do. Children should briefly discuss any ideas with their partner, and then start on it straight away.

Teacher focus for activity

All children: There is much text to read because it tells the story of what is happening. Check that children can read this for themselves, and offer help to support reading skills. Children will need to recognise that some of the data is expressed negatively: 'not free on . . .' 'has to stay home on . . .'. Check that they identify when the children are available from this negative data.

More able and Average: Children should recognise that the most effective way of solving this problem is to draw up a table of when each child is free to play tennis. If children do not begin to do this fairly soon after starting the problem, discuss this with them as a strategy that they might like to adopt. See **Useful mathematical information**, pages 88–89 for a discussion on using tables for solving time problems.

Less able: Encourage children to use a different colour, or a different symbol, e.g. ✔ or ✗, to show when each child can or cannot play.

As children work, ask questions such as:

- *What do you need to find out?*

- *Which days is . . . free to play tennis? How do you know that?*

- *When is . . . not free? How do you know that?*

Optional adult input

Work with the Average group. Help them to draw a suitable table, with days of the week for columns and children's names for rows. Ensure that they understand the differences in the information presented, i.e. when a child can play or is doing something else.

Plenary

Have the outline of the table – names and days of the week – ready on the board, but covered.

1 Invite various children to explain how they set about solving the problem. Discuss the tables or lists that they drew up. Ask:

- *Which do you think shows the time the children are available more easily: a table or a list? Why do you think that?*

- *What are the advantages of using a table?*

2 Reveal the table and discuss how a table, set out like the one below, makes the data easily available, so that it is possible to spot when each pair of children could be free.

3 On the board, fill in the table with the children's help so that all can see it and ask:

- *On which day can Ramesh and May play?* (Monday)

- *On which day can . . . play?*

- *How many matches will there have to be altogether if each of the 4 children is to play the other children?* (6)

Discuss how there will need to be 6 matches:
1 Ramesh and May, **2** Ramesh and Tom; **3** Ramesh and Emily; **4** May and Tom; **5** May and Emily; **6** Tom and Emily.

4 Ask further questions, encouraging children to read off the answers from the table, such as:

- *On which day can no matches be played? Why is that?*

- *Is there a day when more than 1 match can be played?*

- *If you were going to arrange the matches, what would you decide? Why?*

5 Talk about how the information was presented in the problem, for example, that some negative information was given – 'stay at home on . . .', 'is not free on . . .'. Ask children to explain how they dealt with this. Discuss how a piece of negative information has to be interpreted in such a way that it becomes useful. In this example, if a child cannot play on particular days then they must be able to play on the other days.

Development

As an extension activity or for homework, children could develop their data sorting skills by creating their own similar question on a smaller scale.

A further example to try can be found under **Useful mathematical information**, pages 88–89.

Solutions

Children will need a table like this in order to work out when each pair of children can play tennis.

	Mon	Tues	Wed	Thurs	Fri	Sat	Sun
Ramesh	✔	✗	✗	✔	✔	✗	✗
May	✔	✗	✔	✗	✗	✔	✗
Tom	✗	✔	✗	✗	✔	✔	✗
Emily	✗	✔	✔	✔	✗	✗	✗

✔ available
✗ not available

So, the children have the following availability:

1   Ramesh can play May on Monday.

2   Ramesh can play Tom on Friday.

3   Ramesh can play Emily on Thursday.

4   May can play Tom on Saturday.

5   May can play Emily on Wednesday.

6   Tom can play Emily on Tuesday.

The solutions for PCM 20 are the same as for Textbook page 41.

30 Going to the cinema

Minimum prior experience

telling the time; using am and pm; reading simple timetables; Lesson 29

Resources

Textbook pages 42 and 43, PCM 23 clock faces or ready-made clock faces, PCM 21, PCM 22

Key vocabulary

time, am, pm, how long . . .?, timetable, arrive, depart, minute, hour, days of the week

30 Going to the cinema

Lauren, Sarah and Milly are best friends.
They want to go to the cinema together to see the new Pop Star film.
But they are all so busy!
Can you find a time when they can all go together?

Here is what they are doing.

Sarah's Diary
Sunday Football 12–4:30 pm
Monday
Tuesday
Wednesday
Thursday
Friday
Saturday Judo 10:30 am – 2pm

Milly
Sunday Visit Granny 5–8 pm
Monday
Tuesday Swimming 5:30–7:30 pm
Wednesday
Thursday Swimming 5:30–7:30 pm
Friday
Saturday Swimming 2–3:30 pm

Lauren
Sunday Dancing class 1–3 pm
Monday Dancing class 5–8 pm
Tuesday
Wednesday Dancing class 5–8 pm
Thursday
Friday Dancing class 5–8 pm
Saturday

They are at school from 9:00 am to 3:30 pm.
They all go to bed at 9:00 pm on a school night.

42

What's the problem?

The problem involves sifting data in a timetable in order to schedule a visit to the cinema.

Problem solving objectives

- Solve mathematical problems or puzzles, recognise simple patterns or relationships, generalise and predict. Suggest extensions by asking 'What if . . .?' or 'What could I try next?'
- Explain methods of calculation and reasoning about numbers orally and, where appropriate, in writing.
- Solve word problems involving numbers in 'real life', money and measures, using 1 or more steps. Explain how the problem was solved.

Differentiation

The activity on Textbook pages 42 and 43 is for the whole class, but is differentiated by resources used:

More able: PCM 22.

Average: PCM 21 or PCM 22.

Less able: PCM 21.

PCM 21 and 22 provide a timetable for recording, with some information already completed on PCM 21.

Introducing the problem

Ask children to look at the timetable details in their Textbooks. Explain: *The 3 girls want to go to the cinema together. They all lead busy lives. Your task is to work out when they are all free.*

Read through the activity together and check that children understand what they have to do. Provide copies of PCM 21 or 22, which contain recording grids that children may find helpful.

Ask children to discuss with their partner how to begin the activity. Remind them to write down what they do.

Teacher focus for activity

All children: Encourage children to record the data in the timetable by each day, so that they can see when all of the girls are busy. They may wish to use a different colour for each girl. See **Useful mathematical information**, pages 88–89 for a discussion on using tables for solving problems involving time.

More able and Average: Check that children can interpret the times in the timetable and relate them to morning, afternoon and evening. If children find this difficult, suggest that they use the clock faces.

Less able: Children may find the clock faces helpful. Check that they understand what am and pm mean.

As children work, ask questions such as:

- *Who is busy on Sunday afternoons?*
- *On which days are Lauren/Sarah/Milly not busy? How do you know this?*

Optional adult input

Work with the Less able group. They can work in pairs or smaller groups, each group focusing on a couple of days, then put all the days together and discuss the findings as 1 group.

Plenary

Have a blank table, as below, covered and ready to fill in on the board.

1 Ask children how they set about solving the problem. Encourage children to discuss how the problem requires them to find when all of the children are free at the same time.

2 Using the blank table, and with children's help, make a list of the week's activities, listing these on a daily basis. Agree that all of the girls are in school during the weekdays from 9:00 am to 3:30 pm. Agree also that there is no showing of the film during school hours.

They can then use this table and look at the information about film times to see when there is time available for all 3 girls. Children may recognise the layout, as it is like a school timetable.

Ask:

- *Are all the children available to go to the cinema on Monday? Why not?*
- *What about Tuesday? And Wednesday? And Thursday? Explain why they can't go.*
- *Can you see a time when all the girls are free?*
- *Is there 1 day? Is another day possible?*
- *What about Sunday? Is Sunday possible? Why not?*

Development

Children could create their own simple diaries for 3 or 4 children, with similar times and activities and make up their own questions based on the

information, then swap books and try to sort each other's data. There is also a further activity for sorting data with tables in **Useful mathematical information**, page 89.

Solutions

Children should have found that there are 2 possible times for going to the cinema: Friday evening 9:00–11:00 pm; or Saturday 6:30–8:30 pm. You may wish to discuss the impracticalities of going to the cinema on Monday–Thursday or Sunday at 8:30 onwards, with school the next day. Friday, however, might be possible.

Ask children which time they would prefer and why. Suggestions may include:

- Go on Friday because school has finished for the week.
- Go on Saturday because the Friday showing is late and Lauren may be too tired after her dance class.

Congratulate the children on successfully solving this problem.

		M	T	W	T	F	S	S
am	9:00	S	S	S	S	S		Lauren Dancing
	10:00	C	C	C	C	C		Lauren Dancing
	11:00	H	H	H	H	H	Sarah Judo	Lauren Dancing
	12:00	O	O	O	O	O	Sarah Judo	Sarah Football
	1:00	O	O	O	O	O	Sarah Judo	Sarah Football
	2:00	L	L	L	L	L	Milly Swim	Sarah Football
pm	3:00						Milly Swim	Sarah Football
	4:00							
	5:00	Lauren Dancing	Milly Swimming	Lauren Dancing	Milly Swimming			Milly Granny
	6:00	Lauren Dancing	Milly Swimming	Lauren Dancing	Milly Swimming			Milly Granny
	7:00	Lauren Dancing	Milly Swimming	Lauren Dancing	Milly Swimming			Milly Granny
Bedtime	8:00							
	9:00	B	B	B	B			B
	10:00	E	E	E	E			E
	11:00	D	D	D	D			D

Useful mathematical information

These pages provide further explanation to assist the teacher with the mathematics used in some lessons. Each section is referenced to the relevant activity so that it is easy to find what is needed starting from the lesson plan for the problem.

Some sections cover the mathematics that underpins the problem. Other sections cover the specific mathematical concepts that children will understand. Both are intended to be information given for the non-specialist mathematics teacher.

Arrangements in a grid

(Lesson 1)

This arrangement in the grid is just one of many possible responses. For example, the grid can be rotated 90° or 180°. Once the children have grasped that these are the same basic solutions they may spot other solutions.

Grid from Solution page

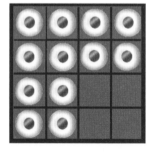

Grid rotated 90°

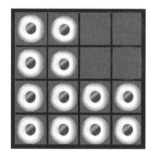

Grid rotated 180°

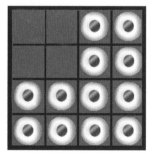

Similar solution

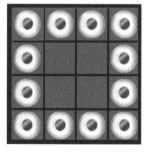

If the empty spaces are kept together in a 2×2 square, this can be moved around the grid, as in the examples below.

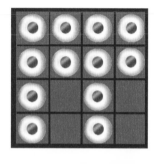

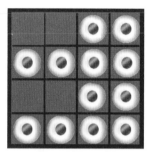

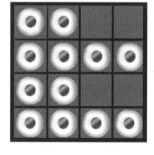

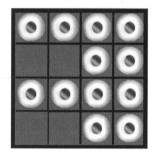

Palindromes

(Lesson 2)

Children may already be aware of palindromic words, such as bib, dad, noon, and so on. They may not yet have met palindromic numbers.

These are the palindromic numbers from 1000 to 10 000. They share a common property: all of these numbers have a factor of 11.

1001	2002	3003	4004	5005	6006	7007	8008	9009
1111	2112	3113	4114	5115	6116	7117	8118	9119
1221	2222	3223	4224	5225	6226	7227	8228	9229
1331	2332	3333	4334	5335	6336	7337	8338	9339
1441	2442	3443	4444	5445	6446	7447	8448	9449
1551	2552	3553	4554	5555	6556	7557	8558	9559
1661	2662	3663	4664	5665	6666	7667	8668	9669
1771	2772	3773	4774	5775	6776	7777	8778	9779
1881	2882	3883	4884	5885	6886	7887	8888	9889
1991	2992	3993	4994	5995	6996	7997	8998	9999

So, for example, $1001 \div 11 = 91$ and $9779 \div 11 = 889$.

Digital roots

(Lesson 3)

The digital root of a number can be found by totalling its digits. The resulting digits are totalled, and this is repeated until there is just 1 digit; this is the digital root.

The digital root of 5496 can be found like this:

$$5 + 4 + 9 + 6 = 24$$
$$2 + 4 = 6$$

So the digital root is 6.

When testing numbers to check whether they are divisible by 9, finding the digital root is a quick way of doing this, because the digital root of numbers with a factor of 9 is always 9.

For example:

18 has a digital root of 9 ($1 + 8$).

369 has a digital root of 9 ($3 + 6 + 9 = 18$ and $1 + 8 = 9$).

Fractions of quantities

(Lesson 4)

When working with fractions of quantities, children need to understand the vocabulary of fractions, for example, half of 18 m can be found by halving, or by dividing by 2.

Similarly, children need to understand addition of fractions with the same denominator to total 1:
$\frac{1}{3} + \frac{2}{3} = 1$

So if $\frac{1}{3}$ of an 18 m rope is thrown away, then $\frac{2}{3}$, or 12 m remains. Children will find $\frac{1}{3}$ by dividing by 3, and $\frac{2}{3}$ by doubling $\frac{1}{3}$ or adding $\frac{1}{3}$ and $\frac{1}{3}$.

Fractions of numbers

(Lesson 5)

Fractions of whole numbers can be found using division.

For example, $\frac{1}{3}$ of 45 can be found by dividing 45 by 3.

$$\frac{1}{3} \text{ of } 45 = 45 \div 3 = 15$$

Division produces equal groups. For example, dividing 45 by 3 produces 15.

$$3 \times 15 = 45$$

Empty number line

(Lessons 6, 7 and 11)

The empty number line is a useful device for calculating addition and subtraction. Children can use this as a way to visualise the operation that they are performing.

For example:

$$46 + 37 = 46 + 30 + 4 + 3 = 83$$

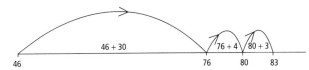

Here the sum begins with the larger number, 46, then the 37 is partitioned into tens and units, with the units partitioned so that another ten can be made, that is $76 + 4$.

Similarly the empty number line can be used for subtraction.

$$83 - 37 = 83 - 30 - 3 - 4 = 46$$

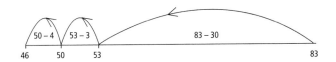

Place value position of digits and totals

(Lesson 8)

When searching for the largest possible total, using given digits, the highest value place must have the largest digits, while the smallest value place must have the smallest digits. For example, for the digits 1, 2, 3, 4, 5, 6 and making the largest HTU sum total:
$$642 + 531 = 1173$$

It does not matter in which HTU number the digits appear, as long as the 5 and 6 are in the hundreds place, the 3 and 4 in the tens place and the 1 and 2 are in the units place.
$$631 + 542 = 1173$$

Where the smallest possible total is needed, then the reverse is needed, where the largest value place has the smallest digits and the smallest value place has the largest digits.

For example, for the digits 1, 2, 3, 4, 5, 6 and making the smallest HTU sum total:
$$135 + 246 = 381$$

Again, it does not matter in which number the digits appear, as long as the 1 and 2 are in the hundreds place, the 3 and 4 are in the tens place and the 5 and 6 are in the units place.

$146 + 235 = 381$

Games of strategy

(Lesson 9)

Games of strategy can help children to become more confident in developing strategies to use in solving problems. When playing a new game which is not just a game of luck, encourage the children to consider:

- What mathematics do I need to use in this game?
- Can I spot any patterns in the numbers I might need?
- How can I stop my opponent from winning?
- What could my opponent do next?

There are many games of strategy available for children to try. Consider setting such games as a homework activity for all the family to play. These games can include, for example:

- Card games where the players try to guess what cards the other player has to stop them from winning.
- Board games, including Backgammon where possible dice combinations, free spaces on the board, safeguarding pieces, blocking the opponent or sending them back must be considered.
- Games available from websites, including those from around the world, such as Mu Torere, which is a blocking game, and Mancala.

Letters on telephone key pads

(Lesson 10)

When using the telephone key pad for numbers and letters, the children may notice the distribution of letters to numbers and wonder about the background to letters on a telephone key pad.

They may enjoy undertaking some historical research about telephones. The children will discover that originally the telephone number for a home consisted of the name of the locality and a number, such as the very famous Scotland Yard one of 'Whitehall 1212'.

The first 3 letters of the word made the first part of the telephone number, followed by some digits.

It became necessary to simplify the system, especially as larger telephone numbers were needed. Then all-digit telephone numbers were introduced.

Today, the letters on telephone key pads have become important again, with text messaging.

Logical thinking

(Lesson 12)

When confronted with a word problem, children will find it helpful to write some number sentences which contain the data already known. In some problems they will find that the data they are given includes 'double counting' where data is repeated, in a different form.

Consider this problem:
10 children are eating their lunch and are discussing the flavours of crisps that they enjoy. 4 enjoy smoky bacon flavoured crisps, 6 enjoy cheese and onion flavoured crisps, and 3 like both these flavours. The others like plain crisps. How many children like plain crisps?

4 children like smoky bacon flavoured crisps.

6 children like cheese and onion flavoured crisps.

3 children like smoky bacon and cheese and onion flavoured crisps.

Children may just add up the numbers without thinking about what the data tells them.

There is 'double counting' in the third line above: these three children who like both flavours have already been counted in the previous lines. So:

$6 + 4 - 3$, or 7 children have already been accounted for.

So, $10 - 7$, or 3 children like plain crisps.

Games with running totals

(Lesson 13)

Strategy games where there is a limit to the numbers to be used to make a given total, either by addition or by subtraction, usually involve spotting a counting pattern. These games can be adapted to use other numbers. For example, start at 0, use the digits 1–9, and keep a running total between 2 players, to reach the target of 50.

Here the key number must be 40: this is 1 more than the maximum addition possible of 9, so whichever player reaches 40 first will win the game.

Now, consider how to reach 40: the key numbers are the decades of 10, 20, 30. Whoever begins second should be able to ensure that they reach 10 first. After that, there is always a difference of 10 between each decade, and with the other player only able to add a maximum of 9, and a minimum of 1, it will always be possible for the second player to win.

Of course, if the first player spots the pattern before the second, and is able to move on to the decade numbers, then they will win.

Multiplying larger numbers

(Lesson 14)

There are various strategies that children can adopt when multiplying larger numbers. Here are some of them.

- **Use doubles:** 50×2, where the child may reason that 5×2 is 10, so that they can see that the double of 50 would be 100.
- **Use doubles and multiply by 10:** 50×20, where the child may reason that 50×2 is 100; 20 can be represented as 2×10, so 50×20 would be 1000.
- **Use known facts and multiply by 10:** 50×3, where the child may reason that 5×3 is 15, and 15×10 is 150, because they know that 50 can be represented as 5×10.
- **Doubles of larger numbers:** 95×2. Here the thinking might be: double 100, and subtract $5 + 5$.

Working systematically

(Lesson 15)

1p	2p	5p	10p	Total
5				5p
4	1			6p
3	2			7p
2	3			8p
1	4			9p
	5			10p
	4	1		13p
	3	2		16p
	2	3		19p
	1	4		22p
		5		25p
		4	1	30p
		3	2	35p
		2	3	40p
		1	4	45p
			5	50p

Systematic working is an important skill to acquire in solving problems. Those who do not work systematically tend to try a 'scattergun' approach, which will not ensure that all possible ways have been covered.

In the lesson, children are encouraged to work systematically, changing one coin each time in order to see the effect that this has on the total. The table opposite shows five coins being changed, one at a time.

By working systematically like this, children can see the effect of making one change at a time. They also keep a check on what they have already done so that they do not waste time repeating attempts.

Repeated addition and subtraction

(Lesson 16)

Both repeated addition and repeated subtraction can be shown on a number line.

Using a number line it is possible to see whether a number will divide exactly, or whether a particular number is a multiple of another.

Where children are unsure of table facts, these methods can be very helpful in finding the solution to a multiplication or division calculation.

Using a number line and repeated addition will also show remainders. For example, when dividing 21 by 5, there are 4 jumps of 5 to 20. 21 is 1 more than 20, so $21 \div 5 = 4$ r 1

Arithmetical or algebraic calculators

(Lesson 17)

There are 2 types of calculator that children may have access to. These are arithmetical or algebraic calculators.

Arithmetical calculators

These are usually the cheaper variety of calculator. Whatever order of input is entered into the calculator is the order in which the calculator will carry out the operation.

So, try inputting $5 + 3 \times 2 =$

If the calculator is an arithmetical one, it will calculate this as follows:

$5 + 3 = 8$
$8 \times 2 = 16$

Algebraic calculators

These tend to be more expensive and have far more functions. They are sometimes referred to as scientific calculators. Here the calculator obeys the laws of algebra and carries out the sum in a specific order. It will do the inputs in the following order:

1 Brackets.

2 Multiply or divide, including 'of' as 6 of 5, which means 6×5.

3 Add or subtract.

You may have been taught to remember BODMAS at school:

Brackets; Of; Divide; Multiply; Add; Subtract.

So, for $5 + 3 \times 2 =$ the calculator will calculate it like this:
$3 \times 2 = 6$
$5 + 6 = 11$

If children are using a calculator to work out calculations where different operations are required, it is important to recognise what type of calculator they are using. If it is an arithmetical one, suggest to them that they break down their calculations into smaller steps and carry out each one separately.

NB: Because children in Year 3 probably will not have met brackets before (it is a Year 5 objective, but also covered in Activity 18) use arithmetical calculators, as these will calculate each step, in turn, from left to right, in the total operation.

Multiplying by an even digit

(Lesson 18)

Where the table facts are not yet known, such as for 6 and 8 times tables, the children can use doubles of existing facts.

For multiplying by 6, multiply by 3 then by 2. Alternately, this can be done the other way round, multiplying by 2 then 3.

For multiplying by 8, multiply by 4 then by 2. If children are unsure of their 4 times table, they can multiply by 2, then by 2, then by 2.

For example:
>   To find 2×6
> $2 \times 3 = 6$
> $6 \times 2 = 12$

and
>   To find 5×8
> $5 \times 4 = 20$
> $20 \times 2 = 40$

or
> $5 \times 2 = 10$
> $10 \times 2 = 20$
> $20 \times 2 = 40$

The effects of doubling

(Lesson 19)

This investigation demonstrates how quickly a number doubled, doubled again ... will grow.

There are 2 versions of a traditional investigation which demonstrates this. In the first, grains of sand are used, in the second, grains of rice.

A king has a chess board. It has 64 black and white squares on it. He sets the following problem: put 1 grain on the first square, 2 on the next, 4 on the next, 8 on the next, and so on. How many grains will there be on the sixty-fourth square?

The answer is enormous! 2^{64} or 18 446 744 073 709 525 000.

Some children may like to find out what the number is with billions, trillions, quadrillions or quintillions and all! There are various 'big number' sites on the internet.

Fractions of quantities

(Lesson 20)

When finding fractions of a quantity the fraction refers to a part of the total number of items. In the problem **Money box** there are two seperate sets of quantities: the total number of coins, and the value of the coins. The problem is about the fraction of the total number of coins, not the fraction of the total value of the coins.

In solving problems like this children may find it helpful to put out the coins to model the problem, and to put them into their piles by quantity, that is the half of the coins that are worth 50p in one pile, and the other coins in the other pile. Children can then see that each pile has **the same number** of coins, but **not** the same total value.

Tables

(Lesson 21)

Where a problem involves data that needs to be sorted, then one of the most efficient ways of doing this is by recording the data in a table. This applies to both numerical data and to data that is expressed in words.

It should then be possible to interrogate the data in the table in order to find solutions.

Combinations of 3 dice scores can be shown in a table (combinations of 2 dice scores give totals from 2 to 12).

		score from 2 dice									
	+	2	3	4	5	6	7	8	9	10	11	12
score from 1 dice	1	3	4	5	6	7	8	9	10	11	12	13
	2	4	5	6	7	8	9	10	11	12	13	14
	3	5	6	7	8	9	10	11	12	13	14	15
	4	6	7	8	9	10	11	12	13	14	15	16
	5	7	8	9	10	11	12	13	14	15	16	17
	6	8	9	10	11	12	13	14	15	16	17	18

From this table it is possible to find how many different ways a particular 3 dice score can be found. For example, 17 appears twice on the table:

$12 + 5 = 17$; or $6 + 6 + 5 = 17$
and
$11 + 6 = 17$; or $5 + 6 + 6 = 17$

Number patterns

(Lessons 22 and 23)

It is possible to produce number patterns through investigating shape patterns, such as these: Pick up sticks and Sticky squares.

Encourage the children to look carefully at the numerical data that they produce. Usually in such an investigation there is a pattern. In these activities there is a regular pattern growth. However, as children become more adept at investigations involving number patterns they will meet growing patterns, such as triangular numbers and square numbers.

The triangular number pattern increases as follows:

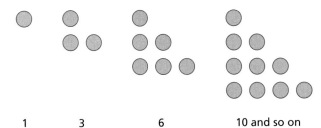

| 1 | 3 | 6 | 10 and so on |

The difference between each pair of numbers increases by 1 each time.

Square numbers form this pattern:

1   4   9   16   25   36 . . .

Note that the difference between each pair of square numbers is odd and forms its own incremental pattern:

3   5   7   9 . . .

More number patterns

(Lesson 23)

Here is an extension activity for children if they complete Lesson 23 quickly or need to develop number pattern skills. It may be used in class or set for homework.

Show children a square as in the 2 previous Problems 1 and 2. Make it into a larger square by adding sticks around it:

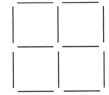

How many sticks have been added to make the larger square? (8)

Do you think you will need to add 8 more to increase it to a larger square? (Children may answer 'yes' because the previous investigations are a regularly increasing pattern.)

Ask a child to draw the new square and ask the class to calculate how many sticks are needed. (12)

Ask children, in pairs, to investigate how many sticks will be needed to make a 5 × 5 square and then the squares up to 10 × 10.
They could estimate how many they think might be needed for 5 × 5 or 10 × 10. Ask them to describe the pattern.

The number of sticks needed each time will be: 4, 12, 24, 40, 60, 84, 112, 144, 180, 220.

Draw the increasing square on the board.

Ask children to explain why the pattern doesn't increase by the same amount each time (because each square is larger than the previous one). Some children may notice that the difference between each increase is 4 (8, 12, 16, 20 . . .).

Reflective and rotational symmetry

(Lessons 24 and 26)

One shape can be seen in different forms using reflective and rotational symmetry.

Reflections

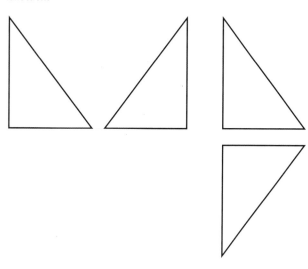

Rotations

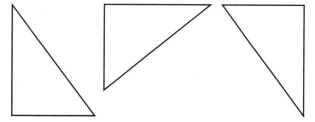

Shape names

(Lesson 25)

The children will be able to make shapes that have 4 to 9 sides. They may ask the names of 2-D shapes with more than 9 sides. These are:

10 sides	decagon
11 sides	undecagon
12 sides	dodecagon

If the children in your class enjoy new words, then they may like to learn these.

There are many websites devoted to 2-D and 3-D shapes that can be found easily with any internet search engine. Children may like exploring them, and also those sites where their questions about mathematics can be answered.

Logo

(Lesson 27)

Children can use Logo for similar activities to Jamie's walk. A maze, or a grid, can be drawn onto an acetate sheet, which can be fixed to the computer screen with Blu-Tack at the corners. Set the children a challenge, asking them to move the screen turtle from one place to another on the maze. If they keep a record of their moves, these can be replicated by another child or compared with the results of others.

When the children are confident with using Logo commands, set a new challenge:

● Draw a house using Logo.
● Put a tree beside the house.
● Draw a car using Logo.
● Draw a sky line view of a city.

Mass and weight

(Lesson 28)

There is much discussion about the difference between mass and weight. Here are some definitions.

Mass is the amount of matter in something and is always the same, whether on earth, or out in space.

Weight is the force with which something is attracted to earth. In space something would have no weight because the forces exerted on it by other stars and planets balance out the force of gravity from earth.

Sorting data

(Lessons 29 and 30)

When faced with information about time that needs to be sorted, a simple table should be used. Once the data is placed into a table, it should then be possible to interrogate the table in order to find some solutions.

With time, the data can be numerical, such as listing specific clock times found in bus and train timetables, or listing words identifying what occurs on particular days of the week.

Development for Lesson 29

Children who require further practice of using a table to sort data could try this example.

Five children want to get together to practise for a girls' and boys' football competition. They need to find an evening when they are free at the same time. Can you work out which day is possible?

Jack could play on Tuesday, Thursday or Friday, but he is normally out all weekend and on a Monday and Wednesday evening.

Amin is busy on Tuesday and Friday, but is free every other evening.

Lucy plays tennis on Wednesday and Friday after school, and goes to visit her grandparents at the weekend.

Fiona could play at the weekend, or Thursday or Friday, but is always busy with homework on the first 3 evenings of the week.

Callum is free every evening except Tuesday and Wednesday.

Solution

	Mon	Tue	Wed	Thur	Fri	Sat	Sun
Jack	✗	✓	✗	✓	✓	✗	✗
Amin	✓	✗	✓	✓	✗	✓	✓
Lucy	✓	✓	✗	✓	✗	✗	✗
Fiona	✗	✗	✗	✓	✓	✓	✓
Callum	✓	✗	✗	✓	✓	✓	✓

✓ = available
✗ = not available

Thursday is the only day when all of them are available. You may wish to extend this further by asking:

Which children could play together at the weekend? (Amin, Fiona and Callum)

Who can play with Lucy on a Tuesday? (Jack)

Is there another day when all the boys (Jack, Amin and Callum) *can play together?* (No)

Our milkman

Draw circles to represent the milk bottles.

Draw the different ways you find.

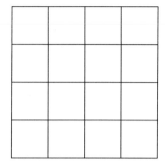
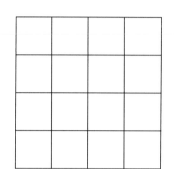
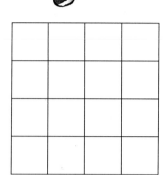

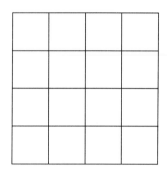
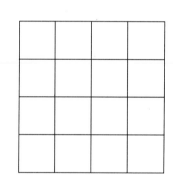
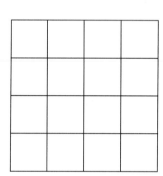

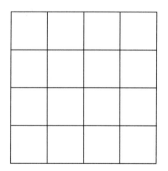
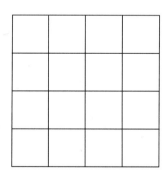

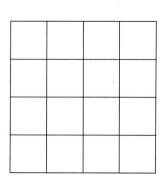
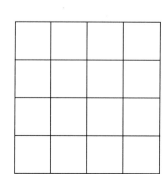

The mysterious dungeon

Record your answers to the riddles.

A (number) _____

(digital root) _____

B (number) _____

(digital root) _____

C (number) _____

(digital root) _____

D (number) _____

(digital root) _____

Now use your digital root to crack the code:

My password

Place value chart

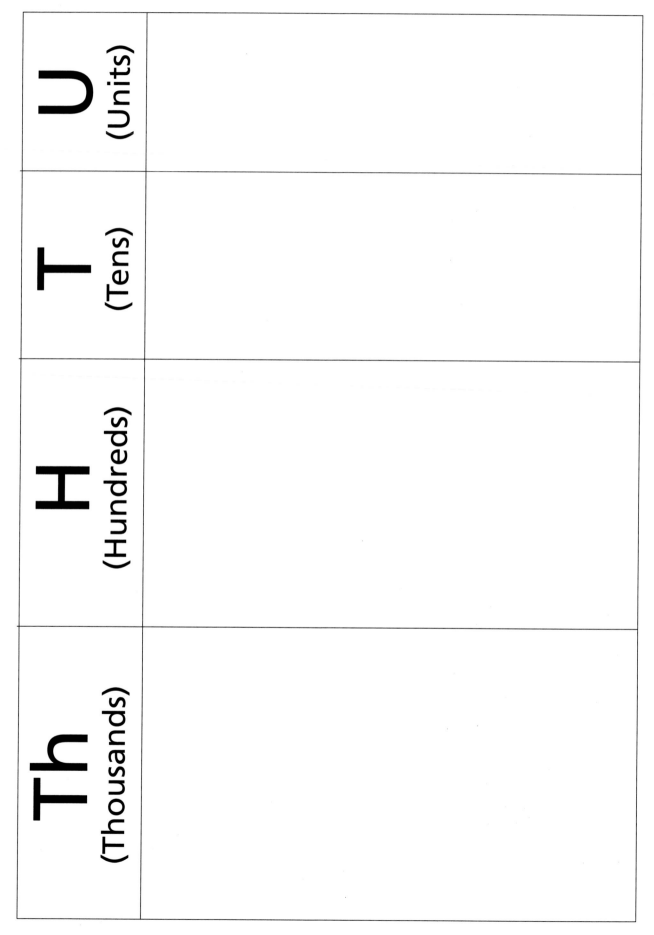

Th (Thousands)	H (Hundreds)	T (Tens)	U (Units)

Empty number lines

Hundred square

1	2	3	4	5	6	7	8	9	10
11	12	13	14	15	16	17	18	19	20
21	22	23	24	25	26	27	28	29	30
31	32	33	34	35	36	37	38	39	40
41	42	43	44	45	46	47	48	49	50
51	52	53	54	55	56	57	58	59	60
61	62	63	64	65	66	67	68	69	70
71	72	73	74	75	76	77	78	79	80
81	82	83	84	85	86	87	88	89	90
91	92	93	94	95	96	97	98	99	100

Close to one hundred

Use these digits and symbols:

1   2   3   4   5   6   +   =

Record your attempts. Try to get as close to 100 as possible.

Calculation	Total

Digit cards 0–9

Largest and smallest totals: 2-digit numbers

Which 4 digits did you choose?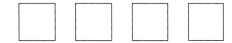

Write your sums here.

☐ ☐ + ☐ ☐ = ☐

☐ ☐ + ☐ ☐ = ☐

☐ ☐ + ☐ ☐ = ☐

☐ ☐ + ☐ ☐ = ☐

☐ ☐ + ☐ ☐ = ☐

☐ ☐ + ☐ ☐ = ☐

Now choose a new set of digits.

Write your sums here.

☐ ☐ + ☐ ☐ = ☐

☐ ☐ + ☐ ☐ = ☐

☐ ☐ + ☐ ☐ = ☐

☐ ☐ + ☐ ☐ = ☐

☐ ☐ + ☐ ☐ = ☐

☐ ☐ + ☐ ☐ = ☐

Write a rule for making the largest possible total.

_____

Write a rule for making the smallest possible total.

_____

Largest and smallest totals: 3-digit numbers

Which 6 digits did you choose? ☐ ☐ ☐ ☐ ☐ ☐

Write your sums here.

☐ ☐ ☐ + ☐ ☐ ☐ = ☐

☐ ☐ ☐ + ☐ ☐ ☐ = ☐

☐ ☐ ☐ + ☐ ☐ ☐ = ☐

☐ ☐ ☐ + ☐ ☐ ☐ = ☐

☐ ☐ ☐ + ☐ ☐ ☐ = ☐

☐ ☐ ☐ + ☐ ☐ ☐ = ☐

Now choose a new set of digits. ☐ ☐ ☐ ☐ ☐ ☐

Write your sums here.

☐ ☐ ☐ + ☐ ☐ ☐ = ☐

☐ ☐ ☐ + ☐ ☐ ☐ = ☐

☐ ☐ ☐ + ☐ ☐ ☐ = ☐

☐ ☐ ☐ + ☐ ☐ ☐ = ☐

☐ ☐ ☐ + ☐ ☐ ☐ = ☐

☐ ☐ ☐ + ☐ ☐ ☐ = ☐

Write a rule for making the largest possible total.

_____

Write a rule for making the smallest possible total.

_____

Total thirty-one

_____ and _____ played this game.

Take turns to play.

Add your numbers to the running total.

Write the sum.

Write the new total.

Name	Sum	Running total
	$0 + \square = \square$	

A pocketful of money

Record the coins on this chart.

1p	2p	5p	10p	20p	50p	Total

Count down to zero

_____ and _____ played this game.

Take turns to play. Use the numbers **1**, **2**, **3**, **4**.

Subtract your number from the starting number.

Write down the subtraction sentence.

Write the new starting number for your partner.

Starting number	Subtraction sentence
⬭ 31 ⬭	⬭ 31 ⬭ − [ ] = ⬭ ⬭
⬭ ⬭	

0	1	2	3	4	5	6	7	8
9	10	11	12	13	14	15	16	17
18	19	20	21	22	23	24	25	26
27	28	29	30	31	32	33	34	35
36	37	38	39	40	41	42	43	44
45	46	47	48	49	50	51	52	53

0–53 Number line

47	48	49	50	51	52	53	54	55
56	57	58	59	60	61	62	63	64
65	66	67	68	69	70	71	72	73
74	75	76	77	78	79	80	81	82
83	84	85	86	87	88	89	90	91
92	93	94	95	96	97	98	99	100

47–100 Number line

Apex Maths 3 © Cambridge University Press 2003

Calculator magic

Start number	Target number	Calculation for target number	Correct?

Which mental or pencil and paper methods did you use?

_____

_____

Ice cream cones

There are 5 flavours of ice cream to choose from:

You want to buy a double scoop with 2 different flavours.

Which different combinations could you choose?

Use the table to record the combinations.

	Vanilla	Chocolate	Raspberry	Strawberry	Coffee
Vanilla					
Chocolate					
Raspberry					
Strawberry					
Coffee					

How many different combinations are there?

Squares and triangles

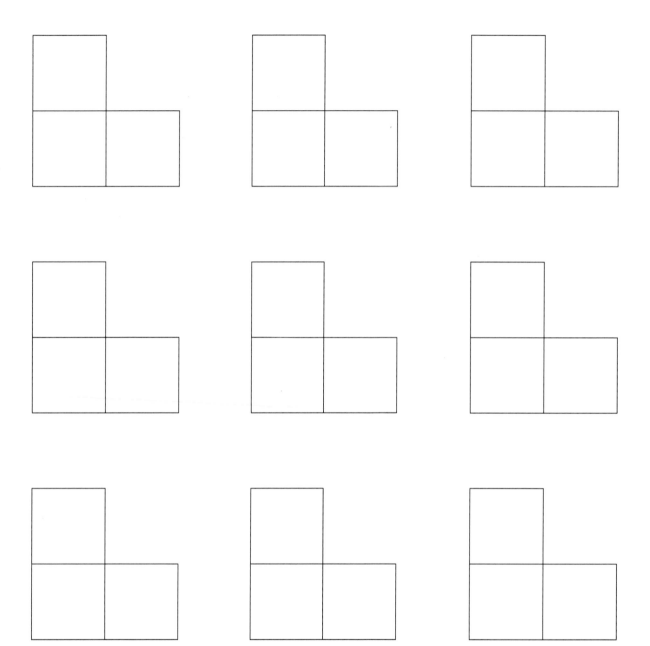

Make that shape

Draw on to these outlines the shapes you used to make them.

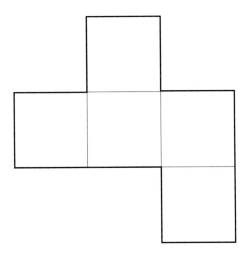

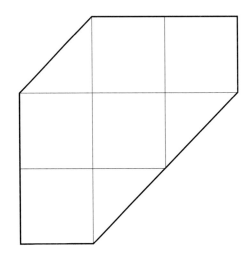

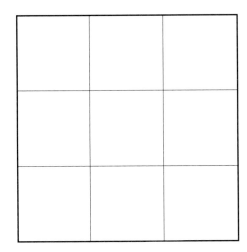

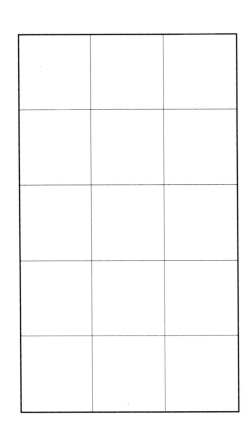

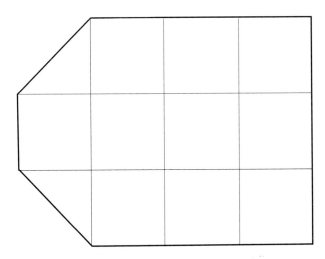

Jamie's walk

Record your routes on this grid.

Use a different colour pencil for each route you try.

Tennis matches

Ramesh, May, Tom and Emily like to play tennis.

They each want to play each other.

Work out which day each pair can play on.

- Ramesh cannot play on Tuesday, Wednesday or Saturday.
- May can play on Monday, Wednesday and Saturday.
- Tom cannot play on Monday, Wednesday and Thursday.
- Emily can play on Tuesday, Wednesday and Thursday.
- None of them can play on Sunday.

Use the table to show when each can play.

	Mon	Tues	Wed	Thurs	Fri	Sat	Sun
Ramesh							
May							
Tom							
Emily							

1 When can Ramesh play May? _____

2 When can Ramesh play Tom? _____

3 When can Ramesh play Emily? _____

4 When can May play Tom? _____

5 When can May play Emily? _____

6 When can Tom play Emily? _____

Going to the cinema

Colour the times when each girl is busy.

		Mon	Tues	Wed	Thurs	Fri	Sat	Sun
am	9:00							
	10:00							
	11:00							
	12:00			At school				
pm	1:00							
	2:00							
	3:00							
	4:00							
	5:00							
	6:00							
	7:00							
	8:00							
Bedtime	9:00							
	10:00			In bed				
	11:00							

When can Lauren, Sarah and Milly go to the cinema together?

_____

_____

Name .... Date ....

22

Going to the cinema

Colour the times when each girl is busy.

		Mon	Tues	Wed	Thurs	Fri	Sat	Sun
am	9:00							
	10:00							
	11:00							
	12:00							
pm	1:00							
	2:00							
	3:00							
	4:00							
	5:00							
	6:00							
	7:00							
	8:00							
Bedtime	9:00							
	10:00							
	11:00							

When can Lauren, Sarah and Milly go to the cinema together?

_____

_____

Clock faces

Photocopy on to card.

Cut out.

Fix the hands to the clock with a paper fastener.

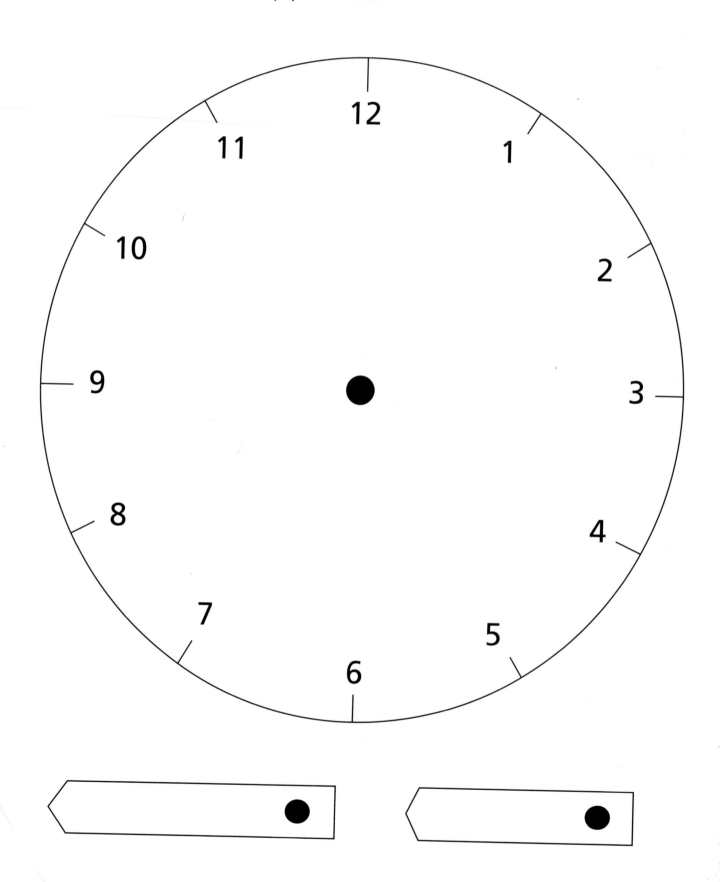